God Meant It For Good: A Cuban Refugee Story

Maria Wells and Joel Wells

Published by Joel Wells, 2024.

GOD MEANT IT FOR GOOD: A CUBAN REFUGEE STORY

First edition. October 1, 2024.

Copyright © 2024 Maria Wells and Joel Wells.

ISBN: 979-8227181350

Written by Maria Wells and Joel Wells.

Table of Contents

Introduction

MY NAME IS MARIA ROSA Baro de la Sierra Wells. I was born on March 23, 1950, into an affluent family in Havana, Cuba. My world changed radically when, alone, I boarded a Pan Am flight bound from Havana to Miami on August 3, 1961, as a part of the clandestine "Pedro Pan flights." At that time, I became an 11-year-old Cuban refugee coming to the U.S. who no one had a plan for but God.

Fifty years later in May 2012 I returned to my former homeland for the first time since my life changing exit from Havana, Cuba. When I visited my childhood home in the Miramar section of Havana God had a gift waiting for me. I was both stunned and overjoyed with it. I discovered it at the beautiful home which my parents built when I was a child. God's gift was a brief reconnection with memories of a wonderful time with my parents and sister and a formerly untroubled life that I enjoyed with them.

Unfortunately, that home is now owned by the Cuban government. Even so, that gift took on a life of its own as it symbolized God's answer to my lifelong question of 'why?' I now could tell this amazing story about God's purpose for me despite the heartache, the grief, the loneliness, and the challenges I experienced after leaving Cuba. It was all a part of God's grand plan which I did not recognize for most of my life. "Why" includes missions, missionaries, and the saving of souls. It includes my oldest son and my eventual connection with and love for the Cuban people living there today. This is my story. "Unete a mi!" (Join me.)

Chapter 1 The Dream

I WAS ON THE BEACH outside the picturesque Yacht Club at Miramar, Havana, Cuba where my parents were members. Instead of my usual practice of swimming and playing on the beach as outside speakers in the palm trees played Vienna waltzes, I was frightened by shooting and explosions. In horror I watched panicking people running for their lives. Then I awoke from my dream only to find out that the sounds of battle were real, and they were close.

Rushing quickly into my mother's bedroom to determine what was happening, I found my mother in her closet feverishly packing my PE bag with my older sister's medicines. Matilde was 15 years older than I and suffered with Schizophrenia. Without looking at me, my mother said, "she might need these." It was obvious to me that something terrible was happening and we might have to flee our home. I loved my home, with its unique coquina rock entrance, indoor rock garden and tropically landscaped lawn especially in the back yard where my tree swing was. Our home was in an exclusive neighborhood in the Havana area called Artura de Miramar.

As soon as "Mommy" was done packing we went into our Florida Room where my mother turned on the black-and-white television set. Overcome with sadness, I watched young, Cuban men with their hands clasped over their heads marching in line at gunpoint to prison. It was April 1961 and as an 11-year-girl I was witnessing the failed "Bay of Pigs" invasion.

It was only a few days later that my mother took me to the American Embassy in Havana. We rode in a cab as my mother did not drive. Once there we went directly to the desk of a friendly, thin, grey-headed man in his late fifties who was the brother of one of my mother's friends. He helped us update my passport. He had me sign it, making me feel very grown up.

My mother was on a mission, but I had no clue what it was. My mother's energy did not seem to match her age of 59 (I was born when she was 48 and my father was 52.) Within days my mother and I took another cab to meet a priest at a Catholic church in a rural area outside Havana near one of our farms. I heard the priest assure my mother that that there would be room on the airplane for me and my aunt Louise. He was speaking about passage for me on a "Peter Pan" flight to Miami on which the passengers would be primarily nuns and children, Cuban refugees. As we were leaving the good priest handed me a light blue colored rosary upon which every bead was engraved inside with a figurine of the Virgin Mary. I treasured this rosary for years.

Once these technicalities had been taken care of my mother's next agenda item was to take me to a shopping area in Old Havana to purchase a "G.I. Joe" like duffle bag. These bags were gray, flexible, and very roomy. Also, during this time we picked up a "traveling suit" for my trip to Miami. My Mom had employed a seamstress to make this special dress for me. It was lime green. The skirt had medium width pleats. The white, short sleeved blouse had white, black and lime green flowers imprinted upon it. It was lovely.

I was not allowed to tell anyone that I was leaving Cuba including the servants or my tutor who had been so nice to me. The warning was given to me as I didn't know who they might tell, and I might not be able to leave the country.

Just prior to my departure, there were final goodbyes to be made to close relatives once again arranged by my mother. We went to see my Grandma Louise, my mother's mom. She lived in a magnificent three-story mansion with a 27-step, marble, staircase, and an elevator. It was always "a happy place" for me and sometimes I found excitement there. One time while visiting Grandma Louise I saw a motorcade arrive and from one vehicle emerged a young dignitary who was there to "court" one of my cousins. I learned later that it was the son of Batista, the president of Cuba at the time.

My Aunt Louise was there the day of my visit to Grandma Louise. Aunt Louise was incredibly quiet. This would be her last trip to Cuba and the last time she would see her mother (my grandmother) and other family members. A visit was made to my mother's cousins who lived across the street from Grandma Louise. They were always good to me, but they were recluses. That day they tried to put on a happy face for me complete with smiles and good wishes. However, I sensed that like me they were puzzled about what was happening.

Everything was now in place for my departure. I did not have a full understanding of what was going on. Questions lingered in my mind like: Who was going with me? How long would I be gone? Since my dad was not a part of any of these arrangements, what did he know about this "trip? I believe my mother would have kept my trip from my dad if she could. To this day I feel sad for my "Papi." He was my hero. I loved riding in his jeep, especially driving around on the farm. On days when there was inclement weather, he would drive me to my elementary school, a Catholic school for girls, La Ursilinas, which was only blocks from my house. (My boy cousins attended La Salle, an all-boys Catholic school in Havana.) During these rides I would tell him about something I would like to have such as a Snow White or a Mickey Mouse toy, and when I got home, he would have it for me. He spoiled me. I enjoyed watching him as he joined his friends sitting around a wrought iron table, smoking Cuban cigars on the patio of our home talking politics. I also loved waiting for him as he returned from a hunting trip at one of our farms. After one of these hunting trips, to my mom's displeasure, he brought to our house one of his hunting dogs, Cinelo. He was a pointer, white with cinnamon-colored spots. Even though we had a gardener, my dad enjoyed working in the yard trimming our mango trees, crotons, and other tropical plants.

It was on the afternoon of August 3, 1961, when my dad drove us in our late 1950's model, Buick, Roadmaster to the Rancho Boyero airport in Havana for me to catch the Pan Am flight to Miami. Aunt Louise, my traveling partner, was also in the car, but my sister, Matilde, was not. Matilde had not accompanied us as she was back at home in her own world. She was so beautiful; I envied her beauty and admired her like she was a movie star. I remember happier times when she let me ride on her back like a horse or had me write on her back with my finger or when she laughed with delight when I made a "granny" face. Then she got "sick" and started taking meds that made her nap often. Her demeanor changed but she was not angry. One time, my mother told me to give her the cards with which I was playing. She explained that I only liked them because they were pretty, and I didn't really need them. I was okay with this request for my big sister even though I didn't understand it.

To me this trip would be an adventure even though I did not know why I was going to Miami this time without my parents. I recalled a previous trip to Miami with my parents and my "nanny" when I was six. I got sick on that trip and my parents sent me back to Havana accompanied only by my nanny. (I have since viewed a U.S. Customs entry of that return flight recording me and my nanny's names in *Ancestry.com*) Even though I got sick I remembered that trip to America fondly. The airport was not terribly busy and going through customs did not take long. The waiting area was an open area, but it was not well lit. All of us sat down on what reminded me of theater seats while we waited for an hour or two until our flight was called. I felt numb, unsure, and lonely. It was like a soundless dream. Nobody was smiling. There was no joy of sharing future activities like one does on vacations. Everybody was going through the motions quietly. However, I was not nervous because I was familiar with this airport having taken previous flights to the U.S. from there.

After a while I asked a female governmental attendant who was watching us where the bathroom was, and she took me there. I looked back at my parents, and they seemed agitated. When I inquired later of my aunt about their apparent concern, she explained that my parents didn't understand why I was being taken away. Shortly thereafter, our flight was called. My aunt and I had to go to the other side of a glass wall to board the plane with other passengers. We were now separated from my parents. I only carried my favorite toy, a doll, with me as we were not allowed to take much with us. Another airport attendant approached me and took my doll from my arms and ripped my doll's head off to search it for illegal contraband that I might have been smuggling. It was an expensive Christmas present from my parents who had brought it back from their last trip to the U. S. After finding nothing the attendant put the head back on the doll and gave it back without comment

Years later I gave that cherished possession to my youngest cousin, Christina, when her family arrived in the U.S. I loved dolls and had a small room in my house in Havana where I kept them. After I left some little girl in Cuba inherited my dolls and toys and maybe passed them down to their children. I hope so.

Soon my aunt and I headed for the airplane. I looked back at my parents who were waving at me. Neither my parents nor I had any idea whether we would ever see each other again but we all expected to be reunited again soon.

I remember a time when my Aunt Louise loaned me a book called *Little Susans' Why's* because I asked so many questions. Unfortunately, there were a lot of questions I didn't ask that day, maybe because I was only 11. Questions like: Why was I really going to America? What impact would the tyrant leader, Fidel Castro, have upon my birthplace, Cuba, the lives of my parents and sister, and my future life? What awaited me in the United States? Would I find new friends like the ones I had in Cuba? What was God's plan for me? I have asked these questions repeatedly over the course of my life, but they didn't seem so important on August 3, 1961 – I was only 11. It was good that I didn't know the answers and it was God's way of letting me down easy.

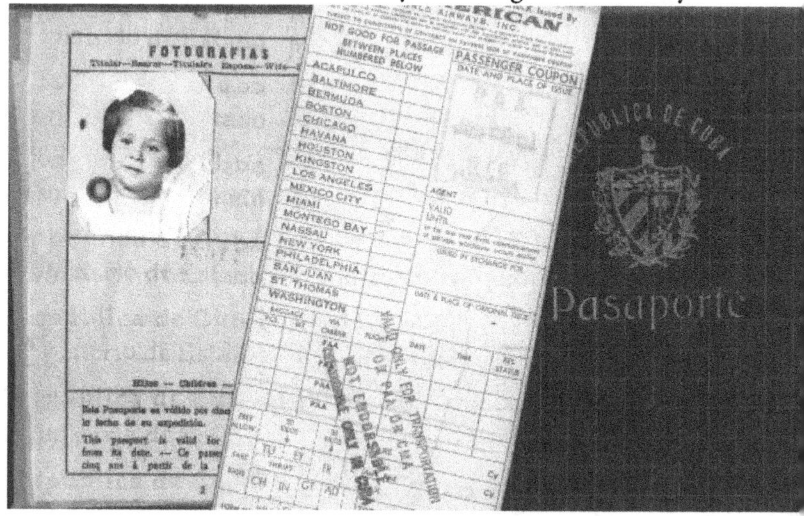

Chapter 2 My New Home: America

ONCE I BOARDED THAT Pan Am flight, I was a part of the historic Pedro Pan flights for Cuban refugees, primarily children and teens. My aunt and I sat near the back of the plane. Looking around I noticed the nuns sitting in front of us. Only Cuban nuns were given a choice to stay in the country so these may have been nuns from the U.S. My sister and my cousins had attended the Merici Academy founded in Havana by American Ursiline nuns which was closed in Havana in 1961. This may have been a group of them returning to the U.S. It was comforting to see the airplane full of nuns. With them aboard what could go wrong? While in flight, the nuns sang religious songs together. It was a short flight of about one hour and soon I saw from the window the blue landing lights at Miami International Airport. The flight had been peaceful, and it was enhanced by the beautiful, blue lights that guided us in at that time of the evening.

After we landed, we went to claim my baggage and they had lost my gray duffle bag. As a result, I had no clothes to wear. (When we arrived at my aunt's apartment in Miami, I had to find some Bermuda shorts and a blouse which I wore for two days until they found my bag.) At the airport we were met by my aunt's grown daughters, Marilys and Isabel., my closest cousins. They came running to meet me and their mother and were shouting "Maria Rosa! Maria Rosa!" They had been in Miami for a while and were excitedly waiting at the airport to take us to their apartment at Tequesta Apartments on Flagler Terrace in Miami. Marilys' fiancé, Manuel, picked us up in his red, American made, convertible and drove us to the apartment which was to become our home for the next year. It was evening and I enjoyed the ride through the big city. Before they left Cuba my cousins had filled my mind with how wonderful it would be in the U. S. and all the neat people, I would meet including Manuel's younger cousin! I wasn't thinking too much about boys then, but this made me a little curious. In any event their preliminary description of my new world was accurate, at least in these early days. I must admit I don't remember much of what they said but I am sure it pertained to all the things they wanted to do and plans for Marelys' upcoming wedding.

My aunt's apartment and my new home was on W. Flagler Street. It was a small, two-bedroom apartment. My aunt and cousins occupied the two bedrooms, and I slept on a rollaway bed in the living room. This apartment complex was not located in the best part of Miami. This was such a difference from the exclusive Havana neighborhoods we had just left. It was true "culture shock" for all of us.

Except for the doll incident and losing my luggage, the first few days of my adventure were without real problems. After claiming my duffle bag of clothes at the airport we returned to our apartment complex. I rushed up to an upstairs apartment where Manuel's cousin and her daughter, Margarita lived. They were my new friends, and my family knew them in Cuba. While I was in their bathroom, I noticed a can of hairspray. Discreetly I sprayed my hair having never used this beauty product. Within seconds I discovered that I had sprayed a portion of my hair gold. Mortified, I tried to take it off with a towel without success. Resigned to the fact I could not correct my misdeed I sheepishly went into their living room where everyone had a good laugh.

New discoveries were a daily event during those first days after my arrival in Miami. My aunt introduced me to the wonder of boiling a can of caramelized condensed milk in water on the stove. We frequently ate this flan-like instant dessert. Another new delight was peanut butter which I had never eaten in Cuba. Our diet was simple. We had to adapt to our new world as none of us did any cooking in Cuba including my aunt and her daughters. We had cooks to prepare all our meals.

Attending school became another adventure for me. Within one month after my arrival, September 1961, I started sixth grade at Citrus Grove Elementary in Miami, a smaller but more modern elementary school than the one I attended in Cuba. This was a public school, and I had only attended a large Catholic all-girls school in Cuba, the Ursiline School. Unfortunately, I did not have any friends to look forward to seeing. Like my school in Havana, my new school was within walking distance of our residence. I recall walking to this new school with a new friend from our apartment complex who was not familiar with where Havana, Cuba was. While walking one day she inquired if I came to Miami on a bus or in a car. Of course, there were new revelations to me as well, such as differences in the meaning of words. On the first day of school the teacher assigned another girl in my class to show me around and specifically directed her to show me where the "restroom" was. Surprised by the teachers' instructions, when my new guide approached me, I naively announced: "no thanks, I don't need any rest right now!"

Everyone was friendly and hospitable at school. Being fluent in English, a benefit of my Catholic school training helped me with socialization. English was one of my best subjects in Cuba, so I was bilingual. I had also studied American History in Cuba, so I had a semblance of an understanding about this new country.

I was thrilled to hear the "Lord's Prayer" over the loudspeaker every day. How powerful and beautiful were those words, I thought. To this day I wonder why any person, court or government would remove that prayer from the classroom. It holds so many promises for humanity. At my Catholic school in Cuba there was obviously a religious component as well. We went to confession, said our "Hail Mary's" and "Our Fathers" which we had memorized, but we were not encouraged to study the meanings of these prayers. I don't recall learning that the "Lord's Prayer" was a model or guide for us to approach our heavenly Father with praise, invoke his will, avow our trust in Him for our needs, and seek His forgiveness and His protection. Different?

Sadly, I didn't get to know anyone very well at this school. After one semester I was transferred to another elementary school, Kinloch Park Elementary, which was about three miles west of Citrus Park. Along with 20 or 30 other Cuban kids I was bused every day to and from this school. Another new experience – riding a school bus.

Novel happenings continued at Kinloch. I learned to sing "Oh Hanukkah, Oh Hanukkah" from a Jewish teacher I had. When we sang this song, I imagined I was surrounded by stars while dancing around a fire with the sky lit up like the Aurora Borealis. Weird, huh? Not really because there was square dancing. What a hoot! It was supposed to be a way to loosen up and make friends, but it was awkward for me when boys joined us, especially Ariel, a Cuban boy in that class who I had a crush on. He also rode my bus.

While I was attending Kinloch, I was invited to a birthday party by one of the students, but my aunt would not let me go. My aunt was being protective of me. She did allow me to go "trick or treating" with other kids in our apartment complex which was the first time I got to join other kids for anything other than school.

As my American adventure continued, I was oblivious to the concerns that would normally accompany a new immigrant due to my age. I was alone but it didn't seem to bother me as visiting with my aunt and cousins in Cuba was common. This seemed similar, only the geography was different. Not only me, but my aunt and cousins, at this time felt like we would be returning to Cuba within a short time. However, about a year later our minds began to change. After window shopping in Miami, my aunt mentioned to me on the bus trip back to our apartment that we should investigate getting a waiver to bring my parents and sister here. By this time, I believe I had already applied for a "green card" which would make me a "permanent resident" after two years residence in the U.S. I assumed that my parents would have no more difficulty than I did to come here, and this "waiver" thing would be just a formality for us to acquire for them.

This same unconcern dogged me regarding my communication with my parents. Telephone conversations between my mom and dad were as frequent as possible, but as an elementary student I didn't understand the dilemma that a "simple" phone call presented for them. Castro had seized control of the telephone system in 1959 when he took power. These telephone calls between Cuba and the U.S. were intensely monitored and controlled by his communist government. Therefore, if I received a call from my parents, it could be interrupted at any time and our conversation would be abruptly concluded. I don't know what "hoops they had to jump through" to call me but through my own experience over the years it sometimes took days for me to just connect with a Cuban operator. Once this operator was given my parents telephone number, I was told that an operator would call back when a connection was made. If I did not receive that call back within five hours, I had to start over and go through the same procedure again if I wanted to make another attempt. Either way, my parents and I were at the mercy of the Cuban government. When I say that they "monitored" the phone call I mean that literally! I was warned by my parents and relatives to be careful what I said over the phone when calling Cuba because "someone was listening."

Taking occasional vacations with my parents, usually traveling to the U.S. was something I was used to. Those early days in Miami seemed like a vacation. However, I would eventually miss my life in Cuba. This included visits to the farm with my best friend, Christina, who I was allowed to invite to join us. Among other things we would ride in my dad's jeep, feed the chickens, and ride horses. Sometimes we went on Sunday, but we would first go to our Catholic church.

But more than the farm I missed having lunch at the Yacht Club. I had been told that our membership was gained through my paternal grandfather who had been a member. He passed away before I was born so I never knew him. Another story I heard growing up in Cuba was that when Batista was president of Cuba, he would come to this yacht club, but due to his mixed race he had to come in through a back entrance. When my mother would take me shopping in Old Havana afterward, we would often go to the Yacht Club for lunch. I remember the mothers would sit in a circle while they ate comparing their stories about such things as needing new carpet, what their life story had been, etc. One mother would bring her son, Raul, who became my friend. With him I would go swimming just off the Yacht Club dock. One time we traded pets. He gave me two parakeets and I gave him a turtle. Seems like I made a better trade.

Another joy was my bedroom at my home, especially my cream and rose bedroom suite. It was a birthday present from my parents. I liked my toys and my books, but I loved my bedroom suite. A rocking chair was a part of this bedroom furniture, and I recall one time that I took my statue of baby Jesus and rocked it while in this chair. I was raised to be a devout Catholic and from a child I had a deep faith, so such acts were not abnormal for me. One time while in a barn at the farm as an eight-year-old I remember praying to God. I thought back then that I was going to become a missionary. However, most of these thoughts of my past life in Cuba were infrequent. Initially, my life in Miami did not yet seem out of the ordinary.

As a result of this carefree mindset, why would the thought of how I was being supported in Miami ever cross my mind? This was something discussed by my mother and aunt in Cuba before we left, but that was a conversation to which I was not privy. (I am sure my dad participated as well, but these two women predominated since they were sisters.) Just before I left Havana, Aunt Louise was given my mother's 3-Carat, solitaire diamond ring. Whether my aunt wore it on her finger as her own at the airport in Cuba or hid it in her clothing I am not certain. I do know that she had it when we went to a jewelry store in downtown Miami shortly after we arrived there. At some point after that visit the diamond ring was sold, I am sure for much less than it was worth, to help pay some of my expenses. My mother had a lot of valuable jewelry and as an adult I discovered my family had connections in Cuba for smuggling it to me in Florida at various times. I do not know if that was transpiring during those early days in Miami. We were already receiving government assistance as Cuban refugees through programs authorized by the President, so we were getting by. But, overnight my residence, schools, social activities, and the people I shared these with had changed. What a contrast from my life in Cuba. Even though I didn't realize it at the time my life was now becoming "Cinderella" in reverse.

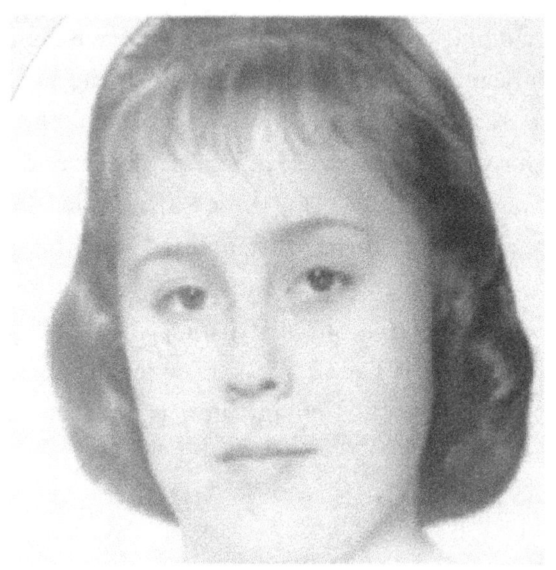

Chapter 3 Gainesville

SHORTLY AFTER THE SCHOOL year ended in 1962 it was decided that I would be accompanying my aunt's family to Gainesville, home of the University of Florida. My cousin, Rafael, was an architectural student there and on his trips to Miami he talked about the area. (Recently he advised my husband that he had influenced our move to Gainesville.) Although still a student he was somehow instrumental in finding a job for my Uncle Broglio, my aunt's husband, in the agricultural department at the University of Florida. We united with Broglio there in the summer of 1962. Uncle Broglio was a chemist in Cuba.

Some years later at a church social gathering in Titusville, Florida, my home for the past 50 plus years, I received an amazing revelation about my Uncle Broglio. One of the men in my church, who had previously lived and worked in Gainesville, began recalling his employment history and the people he worked with. He described an older Spanish gentleman that worked in the Agricultural Department at UF who without a doubt was my Uncle Broglio. The job my uncle held was not glamorous and was not on the level of the work and education level of his job in Cuba, but he set a good example for his children.

The work ethic and drive of my Cuban relatives who came to America was inspiring to me. After living an elite and affluent lifestyle in Cuba they came to the U.S. with nothing. Uncle Broglio's income was low at UF, but he worked hard to provide a living for his family, which now included me. He was like most who fled Cuba after Castro came to power. These were proud, hardworking people who put their family first and who had a heritage that was more important than the size of their bank account. I never heard them complain or seek a handout from the government. I refer to all of this as the "Cuban Factor."

However, due to the sacrifices of their parents their younger family members were able to approach the lifestyle they had enjoyed in Cuba after working their way up the career ladder. My cousins Marilys and Isabel, Uncle Broglio and Aunt Louise's daughters, were among those who accomplished this. Marilys and her husband, Manuel worked at department stores initially in the Gainesville area. After Manuel secured a department manager position at a large department store in Jacksonville they moved there. Before long they moved back to Miami and opened a successful travel agency. One of the last times I visited Marilys before her premature death they were living with their two kids in an exclusive area of Coral Gables. Through their hard work they achieved a lifestyle which included luxury cars, elite schools for their kids, and domestic help.

Her sister Isabel married the son of a successful real estate developer who likewise worked in the same industry and lived an affluent lifestyle for many years. I idolized these two cousins who were like sisters to me. My "Uncle Ralph," my mother's brother, who came to Gainesville a few years after I did, took a job as a maintenance man at Shands Hospital. In Cuba he and his brother, Ramon, raised horses that they raced at Hialeah in South Florida. Uncle Ramon was reputed to have the best racehorses in Cuba during this era.

Uncle Ralph eventually became my father figure in the U.S. during a critical time in my life. I loved this very delightful and resourceful man. It was his son, Rafael, who earned an architectural degree from UF.

After he graduated from UF, Rafael had an illustrious career which included becoming vice president of Warner Communications and the top executive of the New York Cosmos soccer team in 1983. During his tenure with the Cosmos, Rafael was instrumental in bringing Pele to the United States in 1983 according to a New York Times article. So much for family history and the "Cuban factor" let's continue my story of God's providence in my life.

I was oblivious to much of the Lord's handiwork at the time. In any event we moved to Gainesville during the summer of 1962. My aunt, uncle, Isabel, and I moved into an upstairs apartment near University Avenue within walking distance of the University of Florida. This was exciting for a 12- year- old. If we had a car, I do not recall it. We walked everywhere we went in Gainesville – shopping, church, and to the place I caught my ride to school.

I am not sure what conversations were taking place between Aunt Louise and my mother, but my mother's desires for me to have a religious education were conveyed. My aunt was able to arrange for my enrollment at St. Patrick's Catholic School in Gainesville which I attended for the next three years. This school like the school in Cuba had a prominent influence not only upon my life but my belief system as well. I recall in Cuba they would give out gold bows made of ribbon which were pinned on those who earned the highest achievement status. I never earned one of those ribbons, but my friends would ask me to go with them to chapel to thank St. Teresa for their good grades. I still thank God for my little friends who not only had me join them but who also asked me to pray with them during recess to thank God. I was learning more about God and His love for me.

Shortly after our arrival in Gainesville, my Aunt Louise took me to check out St. Patrick's Catholic School and the "Mother Superior." One of the nuns took me to what would be my new classroom. I was entering the seventh grade, so this was junior high school. It is likely that my tuition was free as they understood that coming from Cuba, we didn't have much money. The nuns gave my aunt and I the name of a used clothing store where we could buy my green and white uniforms.

In September 1962 I entered junior high school at St. Patrick's thinking I was ready even though I was nervous in the beginning.

Math was my nemesis just as it was at every school I attended from elementary school through college. This was especially obvious when I had to answer Math problems at St. Patrick's. When called on we had to go to the chalkboard and show our work. This was an incredibly stressful exercise for me especially when you didn't know the answer and how to arrive at it. They say confession is good for the soul so here it is: "I wouldn't have made it through Math if I hadn't been a part of the students in the class who shared their answers." I was so grateful to them and to me they were awesome. I have repented.

I became acquainted with my classmates at this new school quickly. There were only about fifteen students in the class. I was a novelty to them because I was from a foreign country. Everyone wanted to show me around my new school on my first day. This included Mary Anne who has since been my closest friend for life. I believe her father had a Spanish heritage. She was not the only student with a Spanish heritage as there was another one of my classmates who was from Mexico. A hilarious event I still recall was seeing this chubby, little Mexican girl jump from desk to desk to get away from one of the nuns who was chasing her with a ruler because she couldn't answer a question. Likewise, I suffered the ire of the nuns on occasion like the time my knuckles were smacked with a ruler and another time when my mouth was taped. On both of those occasions it was because I did not answer a math problem correctly.

Daily social gatherings in the restroom were a new experience to which I was exposed at St. Patrick's. During this sacred ritual, the girls would talk about boys they liked and would recount their embellished exploits. I thought that these girls were so nice, especially because they were among the students that shared their math answers with me. However, they were a more "worldly" lot than the girls I went to school with in Cuba. If my aunt had not kept a tight rein on me during those years, I might have been more influenced by them as I wanted to be accepted by them. Some of these girls came to my party after I graduated from high school. While a student at the local junior college a few years later, I did not feel the same about them when I was reunited with some of them through my roommate. My college roommate did not attend St. Patrick's, but they were her friends from high school.

I feel like I became Americanized quickly. Rock and roll music, which I had not heard in Cuba fascinated me. It did not have the class of Pop or Broadway music like my parents enjoyed but to me it was liberating. When the radio broadcast my favorite songs, I was no longer alone. I belonged. Alienation was nonexistent when I listened to this music which all my classmates were listening to. Anyway, it was the only thing I could really do at home as my relatives would not let me go anywhere.

I became enamored with the family of President John F. Kennedy, especially Jackie, his wife. I was attracted to the glamor of "Camelot," a royal family, as the Kennedy's were portrayed by the media. Jackie's stylish fashion not only captivated the attention of most women in the U.S. it also seized my imagination. Along with this fantasy perception of the President came the hope that he would amend his mistakes with Cuba at the Bay of Pigs and rescue this nation from the villainous Fidel Castro. How ironic were my conflicting feelings as JFK had let the Cuban people down at the Bay of Pigs and this was the primary reason I was now alone without much hope of reuniting with my parents and sister. Kennedy did experience a degree of redemption following the Cuban Missile crisis. The politics surrounding the Kennedy's were not important to me at the time, however older Cubans who were forced to leave their homeland did not hold him in high regard. (As I grew into adulthood this would become my perception of him as well.)

Then on November 22, 1963, while sitting in my eighth-grade class at St. Patrick's it was announced over the intercom that the President had been assassinated. Despite what other Cubans may have thought about him, as a 13- year- old "resident alien" he was my President, and I was crushed. Amid my adaptation to a completely new country and culture tragedy again struck. In three short years I had seen the government of Cuba collapse becoming a communist dictatorship, I had been yanked from my family and country and now one of my American hero's was dead. I empathized with the tragedy Jackie and her small children were experiencing and was broken-hearted for them.

My parochial school in Gainesville only went to ninth grade so decisions had to be made about where I would attend high school. It was now 1965 and I was fifteen. Castro was still in power so my aunt (in concert with my mother) investigated sending me to another Catholic school but this time not locally. Unknown to me my aunt contacted the Mother Superior at Ursuline Academy of New Orleans, New Orleans, Louisiana, an all-girls Catholic private boarding school which went from early childhood through Grade 12. The school accepted my aunt's request, and it was all set for me to go there. Upon learning about this perplexing development, I wrote a heartfelt letter to the Mother Superior telling her in essence "thanks but no thanks" to what I feared was an effort to make me a nun. I was a good Catholic, but that did not mean becoming a nun was a good decision for me. I recalled again the memory of an eight- year- old child being in the barn of one of our farms in Artemisa, Cuba where I prayed to God and felt a connection to Him. As that tenderhearted child I believed I might want to be a missionary, but as a conflicted teen that dream had faded.

When I consider the circumstances surrounding me, this boarding school would have been a perfect solution to my situation. My parents were locked inside a communist country, and I could not go back there. My closest family members had their own families and lives of their own to live. I was a "square peg" everyone was "trying to fit in a round hole" – their family.

Concerning this dilemma, I am reminded of the classic movie, "The Sound of Music" which was showing at the theaters that same year, 1965. I loved musicals as growing up in Cuba my parents' played records of Broadway musicals constantly exposing me to this genre of music at an early age. This movie fit into that musical category, and I loved singing the songs associated with it. One of the most popular songs was "Maria" which contains the lyrics "How do you solve a problem like Maria?" which in this case applied to me. The irony was that in the movie nuns sang this song.

Could this have been what my family was thinking? For sure my aunt might have thought "What am I going to do with Maria?" She had already raised her two daughters and now she was stuck with raising a teenager who was not her own. No, I was not shipped to New Orleans, and it was nice for my aunt to continue to put up with me for the remainder of my high school years.

Even her two daughters, after they married and moved away, made me feel welcome by treating me like a little sister. They would invite me to vacation with them no matter where they were living, and I have always appreciated this.

In September 1965 I entered Gainesville High School as a sophomore. I look back with fondness upon some events and acquaintances I had in high school. I do not recall having students who attended St. Patrick in any classes at GHS, however I continued my close friendship with Mary Anne. Rock legend Tom Petty sat behind me in 12th grade English class. Obviously, he was not a legend then as his group was in its infancy. I enjoyed high school football games and as was the case with most girls I was thrilled to share classes with football players. I did some dating, but my aunt monitored my extra-curricular activities closely.

While a child in Cuba I discovered that I could draw and paint. I started in elementary school sketching ladies clothing and then progressed to themes that made me happy like ballet dancers and the circus. After I came to America my themes became less hopeful based upon the transitions that that I was experiencing. My art began to portray what was going on psychologically and emotionally within me.

My high school Humanities class teacher liked a "West Side Story" painting of mine and offered to purchase it. I did not sell this painting, and I don't remember why, but it encouraged me to paint what I was feeling on the inside. A later, Picasso-like portrait featuring a two-faced woman painted in black and grey tones reflected the evolving dark feelings of hopelessness that were surfacing in me. Art had become an escape for me, so much so, that upon graduation from high school I chose Art as my major when I entered college.

Unfortunately, there were life changing events unrelated to my being a Cuban refugee that occurred during my high school years. Again, a Humanities class assignment was involved. Albert Camus, a French philosopher, and existentialist was the topic of a thesis I was required to write in this class. After school on a winter afternoon, I rode a school bus to a stop near the Gainesville Public Library and walked the rest of the way there. By the time I finished my research it was getting dark, and I began my trek home with my schoolbooks in hand. It was 1 ½ miles and about a 25-minute walk to my house. As I walked west on University Avenue, I noticed that a suspicious acting man was following close behind me. Beginning to panic I decided to make sure of my suspicions by cutting diagonally across a street which ran perpendicular to University Avenue. It was now about 6:00 pm but it was dark due to the early winter sunset. The man confirmed my fears and followed my path. I quickened my pace and correspondingly my heart rate increased. My assailant quickly charged me from the rear and grabbed my mouth. In absolute terror survival mode kicked in enhanced by surging adrenaline. I bit his hand and instinctively ran into the middle of the street screaming words I had never said before. My books dropped into the street. This was not normally a busy street but fortunately a lady driving a large black car happened by and saw what was happening. I opened her front car door and threw myself into her car breathlessly telling her that a man had jumped me. This "guardian angel" acknowledged this and after a brief pause inquired,

"Are you going to tell me where you live?" My fear subsiding, I was now able to direct her to my house which was only blocks away. With little communication my rescuer dropped me off and drove away.

Once inside the house I told my aunt and my Uncle Ralph what had just transpired. Uncle Ralph immediately said we needed to go to the police station and report this crime. Uncle Ralph drove me there and the police had me look through several books of mug shots. I found no picture that met my recollection of what the man looked like. Nothing could be done further so we got into my uncle's car and drove home. When I returned home, I gorged on food to cope with my anxiety and nervousness.

The next morning as I was entering my Humanities class a female classmate of the same minority race as my assailant the previous night was entering at the same time. She smiled at me and said "Hello" even though I did not really know her. I responded "Hi." I thought how nice of this girl to speak to me. It was like God had put her in my path that day to ensure that I didn't become prejudiced by the traumatic event of the previous evening. As I reflect upon this exchange it dawned on me that this girl and I had more in common than one might suspect. Even though the level of prejudice was not equivalent we both had experienced it. She was an African American, female attending a white high school during the early years of integration in the South. I was a white, Hispanic female student but still a minority who had experienced ostracism and name calling but obviously not to the level to which she had been. Thanks to this sweet young girl I was prevented from becoming bitter and prejudiced by this one incident.

I would not want to go through my "teen" years again. From the time I left Cuba until I graduated from High School, I felt like I was watching a movie of my life. I had no control over it. I was only experiencing it. I was just an actor in a life directed by others. At times I wondered: "God, when will I be allowed to have power over my own life?"

Another transition in my life was about to take place as high school ended. Now eighteen, the prospect of reuniting with my family in Cuba was becoming a distant myth. The oppressive Castro government was growing stronger. Even though my mother's youngest brother, Rafael, had recently come from Cuba, I accepted the fact that my parents would not be coming as they were now in their late 60's. I cannot imagine the heartache that my parents must have felt having suffered so much loss. They had lost everything they owned except our home. From the encrypted letters she wrote me and the occasional "coded" phone calls we were allowed I deduced that they lived in a "welfare state." They received only government subsistence which included walking to the grocery store where the selection of food was limited due to almost barren shelves. Then there was the matter of their two daughters. Their once beautiful, vibrant, older daughter who they lost to mental illness and the younger, "daddy's girl," who they lost by giving her away out of love to another country with hopes of a better life for her.

Gainesville

High School

1968

Chapter 4 College and the Dilemma

AFTER HIGH SCHOOL I worked a couple of part time jobs briefly, but my family urged me to check out the University of Florida for employment. After testing for a job at the University of Florida Research Library I was hired. Primarily I was responsible for filing periodicals and as a result I became more knowledgeable and interested in U.S. and world news. One of the first times I recall having to confront the reality of life outside my world was while I was putting away one of these news magazines. I was shocked by the horrendous cover story about the brutal murder of actress Sharon Tate by members of the Charles Manson family in August 1969. It was an awakening much like the character Dorothy in the *Wizard of Oz* movie expressed when she said, "Toto, I've a feeling we are not in Kansas anymore."

I was excited about this job. My boss was from Cuba as well and she treated me kindly as did all the other women with whom I worked – except on one occasion. Shortly after I began working there, I thought I would show off my understanding of the English language by trying to express my opinion among these older, married coworkers. I announced to them, "You know America is not perfect, but it is the best country ever." One of the ladies angrily interrupted after she heard only the initial portion of my statement by telling me, "Then go back to Cuba if you don't like it here!" It was a lesson learned in appropriate communication skills (during that era.) My youth and inexperience were exposed. My intent was to express how wonderful the U.S. was, and I feel that way even more so now, but obviously it didn't come out that way. Sadly, in our country today, some would applaud the negative in that statement and not even acknowledge the positive.

To further my education, in 1969 I enrolled at Santa Fe Junior College in Gainesville. I applied for and received educational funding through the Cuban Loan Program. Initially I took two classes. My plans were to obtain an A.A. degree and then transfer to the University of Florida where I would major in Art. My social life began to expand now that I was out of high school. One of the ladies with whom I worked at the library set up a date with her nephew. He was a sailor. We began dating. After making a trip to Mexico he brought me back perfume. A few days later I went to a drive-in movie theater with some of my new college friends to see "The Graduate." Like kids in the 60's trying to get away with something I crawled into the trunk of the car and got in free. Later that evening I noticed him at the snack bar – with a date! After this I began starving myself believing this would make me more attractive.

Continuing to work and attend college I became acquainted with a girl named Jenny who was in one of my classes at Santa Fe. She was kind and welcoming to me, so we became friends. Shortly thereafter she asked me to move into an apartment with her as her roommate had recently moved out. The apartment was one block from Tigert Hall, the University of Florida Registrar's office. These were private studio apartments rented primarily by UF students due to its convenience to campus. This was a coming of age for me as I had never lived apart from my family.

After moving in Jenny invited me to her parent's home in nearby Melrose. I had a wonderful time swimming and spending the day with Jenny and her parents. Getting away like this was such an enjoyable departure from the routine life I had been living, I thought. The reinvention of Maria had begun.

One evening I went to the "TV room" of the apartment complex. A couple of guys who were residents and students at UF came in. We got acquainted. I found out that their names were Joel and George, and they were from rural Ocala. In other words, they were country boys.

George was a Gator football "walk on" who played linebacker. The only light in the room was the television so we couldn't see each other very well, but they seemed nice. What I didn't know, but learned later, was that they had been Jenny's next-door neighbor with her previous roommate. Jenny had moved to a bottom floor apartment just before I moved in with her.

Jenny loved to cook and decided one evening to practice her culinary skills on me. Playing social director she said, "Maria, I am locking the door while I cook so go upstairs and visit with Joel and George." I was happy to comply as I knew they were safe and fun to hang around. Yes, they were "safe," but they pulled a prank on me that day which taught me a lesson that Southern boys have a unique sense of humor. Quite an inauspicious beginning to my friendship with these two "nice" guys, one of whom I would eventually marry.

It was not long after that when I began dating Joel. In the beginning he had no idea that I was Cuban. Because he didn't detect a Spanish accent and could not see me in the dark that first night in the "TV Room" he had no cause to believe I was from a foreign country. I was the first Hispanic he knew, and he was extremely impressed that I was bilingual. Remember he was a country boy – an educated one, but still a country boy.

I enjoyed getting to know Joel better. He was a soft-spoken, tall, skinny, redheaded, and freckled face kid who had just turned 21. I had known boys with dark hair, a few with blonde hair but not many with red hair and freckles. He was different and it drew my attention to him. From the beginning I thought he was funny, kind and very handsome. This was during the Vietnam era of American history and students fell into two basic categories - Hippies and Preppies. Despite his rural roots, he was a "Preppy" - a neat, stylish dresser who wore Gant button-down collared shirts, coordinating slacks and either burgundy penny loafers or grey/brown saddle oxfords with or without socks. His misleading "Howdy Doody" looks and timidity belied his ferociously competitive nature, especially in sports. He was athletic and actively participated in intramural sports at UF. To say that Joel loved the Florida Gators, and the LA Dodgers would have been an understatement as he had followed both since he was six years of age.

I recall our first date to a fair on campus. I tried to impress him with the outfit and accessories I wore but I did not make the right impression when we rode the Ferris Wheel. Terrified, I screamed at the top of my lungs for them to stop the Ferris wheel after one or two rotations. Joel assured me that was not possible, but this did little to reassure me. Not a favorable beginning to our romance, was it?

Joel took his studies at the University of Florida as well as his work at the UF infirmary very seriously. He was majoring in Psychology after changing his major from Pre-Med. When he went home for the summer, he worked full time at a sawmill. He used the money to pay his tuition, apartment rental, car payment and other school expenses. He did all this and still found time for me. During the summer I visited him a few times at his parents' home in Fruitland Park. My mode of transportation was the Greyhound bus since I did not drive. I still remember Joel's happy face when he picked me up for the first time at the bus station in Leesburg, near his parents' home in Fruitland Park.

Joel came from a Christian family, and he was the son of a United Pentecostal preacher. He was the second of five children and was the only one who did not attend Apostolic Bible Institute, St. Paul, Minnesota. As a "lapsed" Catholic at this time, I did not have a clue what Pentecostals believed. Over the next couple of years that would change.

On this first visit I was a little nervous but excited. I got to meet all his family as I stayed at his parents' home where his two younger brothers, Larry and Kenneth, and his younger sister, Benita, also resided. His older sister Sandra was married but lived in town with her husband, Robert, who was the assistant pastor. While there I learned to say grace before every meal and each night to listen to the entire family read the Bible and pray before bed during their family devotion.

On one visit Joel had to pick up kids for Sunday School in their nine-passenger station wagon. Even though he wasn't a practicing Christian he did this out of obedience to his dad. Joel did not like this Sunday morning duty and assured me that once he finished college and moved away, he would never do this again. (Untrue as this experience paved the way for us leading a bus ministry years later.) At the time I didn't know what to think about all this church activity which was alien to me.

I was shocked but in a good way by my first exposure to a Pentecostal church service on that initial visit to Fruitland Park. The white, wood frame church building with a tall steeple was a former Methodist church and it was beautiful both inside and out. It had a wood beam ceiling which hovered over the congregation who sat in wooden theater seats. Obviously, their form of worship was much different than I was used to in the Catholic church. I attended, but I was comfortable.

Returning to Gainesville that Sunday afternoon, I resumed my summer routine of working at the library and taking summer classes at Santa Fe. I stayed alone in my apartment for a while, but my roommate went home and did not return. Once my quarterly rent became due, I returned to my uncle's house. My studies and work continued.

In the fall Joel returned for his senior year, but he had a new apartment with two new roommates, one of whom was Cuban. Due to Joel's love for football, I became an avid Gator fan especially after the September 21, 1969, Houston Cougars football game. This was the first Gator game I attended with Joel and afterward we attended every home game over the next two years. It was special for both of us. For him, his childhood hero and sports mentor, his Uncle Joe, a Florida Gator alum, attended the game on a ticket Joel and his brothers had purchased for him. For me, I found a hero, Carlos Alvarez, a

Cuban-born wide receiver, who on the third play of the game caught a 70-yard pass from quarterback, John Reaves, launching Alvarez' All-American season. He was dubbed the "Cuban Comet." He was the same age as I and came to the U.S. around the same time as I did. Unfortunately, Alvarez later became a part of the anti-establishment movement on the UF campus, which was his right, but it has always puzzled me. His family experienced the same oppression as mine before coming to the U.S. but during the Vietnam era he vocally opposed the country to which his family had fled for freedom. To this day he holds positions that are contrary to most Cubans who fled from Communism.

Around Thanksgiving in 1969 I was a guest at Joel's house again. During that visit I joined him and his brothers when they went duck hunting. No, I didn't carry a gun and to this day. I still pray that Joel will not kill any ducks whenever he goes but these prayers have never been effective. It was another enjoyable weekend.

Upon returning home from this delightful time with Joel and his family I had a new dilemma to face. While walking home from work I noticed one day that I was a little hungrier than normal. There were other obvious indicators that aroused my suspicions as well. I didn't say anything about it to my aunt and uncle. I decided to schedule a visit to a doctor's office which was nearby. Since I had no car, I walked there. Working as a receptionist for this doctor was a girl I went to high school with, so I was a little embarrassed when I checked in. I was scared and alone. The doctor confirmed my fears by revealing that I was pregnant. Once again, my world was about to change dramatically, and I didn't know what to do. I needed to talk with my parents, but they were in Cuba and contacting them would take days.

Not long after this I walked over to Joel's apartment and informed him. Not one for showing emotion, I could not tell what he was thinking. At that time, he made no comment about our future. His silence was not reassuring that day.

Later, I did tell my Uncle Ralph that I was pregnant and without condemnation he put me in his lap and hugged me just like a loving father. I loved that kind and generous man. Days later, in my defense, he drove me to Fruitland Park to meet with Joel's parents strongly urging that Joel and I should be married.

Over the next few days decisions had to be made, most of them made by me. After my doctor's visit, the only thing I knew to do was to walk to my Catholic church. There were no people around and no services taking place that afternoon. Entering the sanctuary, I sat on a church pew and asked God, "What should I do?" A voice inside me said, "You are responsible." I was a little shaken, but I wasn't going to ignore this voice as I sensed it came from God.

Next, I went into the church secretary's office and explained to her my situation. She made several inquiries of me which strangely included "What is the color of your boyfriend's hair?" She responded "Oh, you may be having a red headed baby!" I said, "I am keeping this baby!" I thanked the lady for her time and ran out of there as quickly as I could.

Upon learning our predicament one of Joel's friends offered an extreme solution – abortion. It was not even legal as Roe vs. Wade was not decided. His friend seemed well informed on this topic. He said Joel and I could tell our families we were going to a football game and during that time have the procedure performed and return the same day.

During that same week I was in the living room of my uncle's house and surprisingly found a local newspaper lying around which to my knowledge had never happened. Upon picking up the paper I was immediately drawn to an article about "abortion" and the types of procedures. I was horrified by what I read and if there had even been a remote chance that I would entertain this procedure it ended at that moment. I have wanted to write to that newspaper and thank them since that day. Unfortunately, today such a letter would not be well received as a compliment by many newspapers in America.

Based upon my "words from God" and this newspaper article, I told Joel that no matter what he decided I was going to keep this baby! By this time, the fall semester had ended. Joel said when he went home, he would talk this over with his parents, which he did. It was during this time that Uncle Ralph and I met with Joel's parents while he was at work. By the end of December, we had decided to get married, which is a decision we have not regretted for 54 years. Even though we love our three children equally there was a future spiritual element connected to this decision.

Chapter 5 New Beginnings: Marriage and Salvation

AFTER THE DECISION to marry was made, in whirlwind fashion we pressed forward with our plans to marry over the Christmas holidays. We got blood tests. We purchased rings. I went downtown looking for an appropriate dress to wear for the wedding. I went to Wilson's department store where my cousin, Marilys, worked. I wanted an off-white dress, but I couldn't find one, so I picked out a light pink dress with a bow at the neck. Next, I went across the street to Butler's shoe store where I purchased a pair of white dress shoes.

I was now living with my Uncle Ralph and his wife Amelia. She invited some of their Cuban friends that lived nearby to our reception at their home after we returned from the courthouse. This included a friend of Uncle Ralph who was a witness at the courthouse when we were married. These were nice people. Also, Marilys, her husband, Manuel and their daughter, Annette, were present. I am sure Marilys played a part in the planning for the reception. They had prepared a small wedding cake, punch, and finger sandwiches. I was pleasantly surprised, and I was very thankful. It was all genuinely nice.

Afterward we spent the night at Joel's off campus apartment that he shared with two roommates who were home for the holidays. The next day we moved into a furnished 3-room duplex apartment which was our home for the next year while Joel finished his Senior year of college. I resumed my work at the UF Research Library. I dropped out of Santa Fe Junior College so I could work full time. Joel continued to attend UF as a full-time student while working part-time at the Student Infirmary. During the summer he began working for an Ocala construction company that was erecting the new Music Department building. His uncle hired him as a laborer as his uncle was a foreman on that job. Joel continued his employment there until he graduated, and we moved to Titusville.

Two months before our baby was due, I took a leave of absence from the library to prepare for his birth. At work they gave me a baby shower before I left. An extremely sweet Jewish lady who worked in my area of the library arranged the shower. I remember she gave me a blue, baby, bathtub. I received nice gifts.

July 25, 1970, Joel Leon Wells, Jr. was born on the day the doctor predicted. Joel's mother was there for the delivery and stayed with me the week after. Joel's youngest sister Benita stayed for an additional week.

From that day forward Joel's mom was called "Grammy." This was her first grandchild, and she liked the name "Jody." Joel wanted him to be a Jr. so we compromised naming him after his dad and nicknaming him "Jody." From his birth forward I always called her "Grammy."

Grammy was a positive influence in my life. She had raised five children and always had good advice for me. Sometimes she was very blunt as she was a woman of few words. For example, while I was going through labor pains, she reminded me that this was all the fault of Eve. This may have been true, but it was not very comforting at the time. Obviously, my mother was not available, but God provided me a surrogate mother. After spending all that day in the hospital Jody was born at 11:30 p.m. and my life changed forever.

When I came home with Jody, I began my new adventure as a mother. Grammy told me I was too stressed, and she was right. I didn't want to do anything wrong. I even had to ask her about cooking from recipes. I was ridiculous, even making French fries was a challenge to me.

Even though Joel's family didn't participate in the wedding they began to warm up to me, especially after Jody's birth. An example was

Joel's sister, Sandra, throwing me a baby shower at the Fruitland Park church.

The summer ended and Joel returned to school for his final term. I couldn't get my job back at the library, but I was able to secure a position at Shand's Teaching Hospital in medical records. Joel continued working part time on the Music building. He began interviewing prospective employers through UF career services during this last term realizing that upon graduation he had to decide on a job and a permanent residence for us.

In December 1970 Joel graduated. He accepted a job offer in Titusville, Florida as a probation officer with the Florida Probation and Parole Office. In February 1971 we moved to this small town of about 30,000. We finally settled into a duplex apartment at 114 Brown Ave, one hundred yards away from Calvary Tabernacle, United Pentecostal Church, the same denomination as Joel's family. What are the odds?

Shortly after our relocation to Titusville I told Joel that I wanted us to take Jody to church. My Catholic training had taught me "take your children to church." I believed we had a special little boy, and I wanted him to experience God in his life. In response to my request, unenthusiastically, Joel suggested the church across the street, and I said "Fine!" Every Sunday morning thereafter, we walked across the street to church. I know that Joel's parents were praying for us as within days of our arrival Pastor Charles Abernathy and his wife were at our door welcoming us to Titusville and church.

In July of that year Calvary Tabernacle began holding a revival with Rev. Jerry Walton who we had met on one of our visits to Joel's parents' home in Fruitland Park. Brother Walton came by our apartment during the revival to invite us to services. Joel played in a local softball league two nights per week and during those nights in our living room I would watch people coming and going from the church. There came a point that I couldn't stand it any longer, so I decided to check out these revival services and the people who were so happy. Jody had just turned one, so I loaded him into our stroller and rolled him across the street to attend church.

I was so excited about what I heard and felt in these services. They talked about being baptized in Jesus Name and about the Holy Ghost. Before I knew it, I got baptized and the next night I found myself at the altar with my hands raised asking Jesus to give me "this Holy Ghost." I was thinking, "if this becomes number one in your life, the Lord knows your heart and you will receive your heart's desire." I received lots of encouragement while praying especially from Sister Inell Burns (still in our church) who was repetitively patting me on the back because I think she felt that if she stopped praising Jesus everyone around me would stop.

Everyone has their own experience receiving the Holy Ghost so here goes mine. With my hands raised and Sister Burns respectfully hitting my back, I prayed "in Jesus Name' over and over. I pictured Jesus praying in the Garden and then saw him on the cross and this voice inside me said "I did this for you." Immediately I started speaking in tongues. What a wonderful experience! That same weekend Joel quit fighting God, repented, received the Holy Ghost, and was baptized in Jesus Name.

I remember shortly after my Acts 2:38 encounter I had to be sure this was right. I went to the public library and found a Catholic Bible. I do not recall ever reading a Bible in the Catholic church but to make sure these people had not "sold me a bill of goods" I searched that Bible for Acts 2:38. "There it is!" I said when I found it. Now I was convinced that everything that had happened to me was real.

It's amazing all that has happened to me and my family since that time. I have never regretted taking that first step that led to my husband and later contributed to all my children obeying the plan of salvation. Since that day it has been a blessing living for God and letting Him use me in so many ways. My motto is: "Don't belittle yourself as not being important to God and don't ever give up on your family!" I have had the privilege of working alongside Joel while God uses us even though I am not a preacher's wife. I have been so pleased to see my kids become beautiful singers, incredibly good Bible quizzers, effective soul winners and now one is my Pastor -The little one-year-old boy I pushed in his stroller across the street to the church he now pastors.

My four grandchildren have been benefactors of my decision as well as all are actively in the church. I am so proud of all of them. I recall attending my only granddaughter's high school graduation. She was born in China under a communist regime in which unwanted female children like her are placed in orphanages. My daughter and son-in-law journeyed to China in 2005 to adopt her and bring her to the U.S. at the age of 13 months. My daughter challenges anyone in this country who supports diminishing any of our freedoms to talk to her daughter or talk to her mother both of whom escaped the tyranny of totalitarian governments. She proclaims how both received divine intervention to a better life and were able to come to America after their homeland opened the door for them to come to the U.S. When I saw Savannah graduate, I teared up as she marched forward and graduated with Honors. Her name was announced as "Savannah Noelle Jian Sanders" which includes her family name (Jian) at birth. It caused me to cry for her mother and father who gave up their child to a better world never to see her again just as mine did. Our parents sacrificed so we could enjoy these milestones in our lives that they were not able to enjoy with us.

Chapter 6 Citizenship, Hope and Despair

MY LIFE AS A MOTHER and child of God began to evolve quickly. Our church in Titusville was small with an average attendance of about 45. Joel became the youth leader and a Sunday School teacher within a couple of years. He got involved with the teenage boys especially playing sports and hunting with them. I supported him but as a new mother I had to focus on Jody. There was a ten-year-old girl in the church who I took an interest in. She liked Jody so I would take her with us to Youth Rallies and other non-church excursions as she felt like she was taking care of him.

While Joel was immersed in his job as a probation officer, I was a stay-at-home mom. Early on we established two goals for our children: to get them to Heaven and keep them from sitting on the other side of Joel's desk as a probation officer. We believed that the best way to accomplish this was for me to be at home with them and model Deuteronomy 6 during the daytime hours.

We were actively involved in fund raisers for such things as expanding the church by buying the house next door for expansion, Sheaves for Christ, Mothers Memorial, etc. In our personal life I became determined to buy a house because we were throwing away money for rent. I contacted a real estate agent against Joel's wishes as he didn't think we could afford one. However, this agent believed he could get us approved for a special FHA program and he did. We bid on a small three bedroom/one bath house and after we were selected, we believed it was an answer from God. It was listed in the newspaper that we won the bid, and I was so happy. That was in 1973.

On October 27, 1977, I became a naturalized citizen of the U.S. after a five year process which involved trips to U.S. Immigration in

West Palm and Miami, testing my knowledge of U.S. History and an interview by naturalization personnel regarding my willingness to support this country even to the point of bearing arms in its defense. Then on the above date at the U.S. Courthouse in Orlando, Florida I appeared along with a group of naturalization candidates before U.S. District Judge John Reed and was sworn in as a U.S. citizen. Judge Reed was one of the judges that Joel worked for in his position as a U.S. Probation Officer. Joel was present at the ceremony and the reception that followed. No longer the only one in the family who was not a citizen, I felt incredibly good about this accomplishment. I gained a new appreciation for this country through this process and see myself more as an American than a Cuban today. It is admirable that many immigrants are trying to come to this country for a better life, but I would rather they come here legally. Investing in the naturalization process creates a great love and respect for America.

Slightly over a year after my naturalization ceremony, I was getting ready for a mid-week church service when I received a phone call from a relative. It was heartbreaking news that my father had died. He had died a few days before receiving this notice. I was sad, and I recall that evening going to eat after church. As I was waiting to eat, I condemned myself for this as it was the day that I learned my father had died. A letter from my mother some years later indicated that the date of his death may have been in December 1978. Such was the case with each member of my family living in Cuba. I never learned the exact date of their death. My mother genuinely loved my father who was a pushover for his two daughters. I heard one time from relatives that he spoiled my sister by going out during the evening to get her special food while everyone else was eating a delicious meal she didn't like. As I stated earlier, he always wanted to make me happy or surprise me with a gift or trinket. I cannot remember anything bad about my father. As a child I fondly recall the one time my parents got into an argument in front of me. I scolded them and made them make up. They quickly complied. Unfortunately, my desire to see my dad again did not happen. Following my father's death my mother became extremely motivated to come to the U.S. to reunite with me.

I was so happy to see my mother's excitement about the prospect of coming to the U.S. In her communications to me (phone and letters) it was so thrilling to hear that she was praying and seeking the will of God for what was becoming her dream. With the possibility of my mother and sister coming from Cuba to live with us, Joel and I began to plan for this. It was agreed that I would return to college to finish my degree in Education as we would need additional income to support them. However, the plan was for me to take classes while Jody and Steph were at school and during the evening when Joel came home from work. This way one of us would always be home for the kids. We had just moved into a new four-bedroom home so we had room for at least a temporary place for my mother and sister to stay until we could find them a place of their own.

With the credits I had earned at Santa Fe Junior College in Gainesville it didn't take long for me to earn my AA degree in July 1979 from Brevard Community College. I then enrolled at the University of Central Florida (UCF) in their elementary education program at their Brevard campus in Cocoa. I tried to go full time and rush home from class for Stephanie who I placed in daycare for one hour per day. That did not work because Stephanie cried the whole time for me. I couldn't take it so I asked for permission to be a part-time student so that I would be home when they both got out of school.

The department head of this program at UCF was not happy with my request. She intimated to me that I should put my studies above my children at least during the time of my education. Although she consented to my appeal, she did not make it easy on me in my classes, especially during an internship. I continued until my Senior year making good grades and even was asked to join an academic fraternity at UCF. However, the stress of being a student-mom affected me not only emotionally but physically as well. I decided to drop out during my Senior year and Joel agreed with me that we would trust God as it was not our initial intention for me to be anything other than a stay-at-home mom.

In December 1978 my mother's efforts began in earnest to reunite with me. The U.S. Interest Section in Cuba opened in 1977 as a replacement for the American embassy since diplomatic relations between Cuba and the U.S. had ended. Some of her letters referred to the "Interest section." It is obvious that she became aware of this and educated herself through her interaction with the interest section. Possibly the same friend she had at the U.S. Embassy in Cuba who helped me enter the U.S. was still there. In any event she guided Joel and me through the steps we should be taking in the U.S. Joel submitted financial documents every six months to the State Department as requested by this agency plus written assurance that we would be responsible for their support once they arrived in the U.S. You will note that my mother questions at times our understanding of our responsibility.

Now I am going to introduce you to Maria Francisca de la Sierra-Baro up close and personal through some of her letters she sent to me between 1982 – 1985. The first of these letters was written when she was 80 years old. You will learn that she was a highly intelligent and resourceful woman who often used coded language on the phone and in her letters. Also, it is important to understand what was going on in Cuban American relations during the time of these letters. Following the "Mariel Boatlift" in 1980 initiated by Castro and the subsequent influx of refugees from Haiti, in 1980 the U.S. reduced the worldwide entry into the U.S. of refugees and immigrants annually to 50,000 and 270,000 respectively. Therefore, limitations were being placed on the number of foreigners who would be able to get into the U.S. The following are some of the letters she sent to me which were written in Spanish, but I have translated them into English for the reader:

September 2, 1982

Daughter, we really remembered you on the day of your feast day which is August third ... I suppose you have received the cable (about my feast day) that we sent to you even though I know you don't celebrate it. I must do it as I cannot leave it undone. We always think of you. Please I beg of you do not make any comments about the problems of Madrina (code name) because it's not good. It's not healthy to talk about problems. Tell me if my friend Mercedes (another code name) called. Tell her "Hello" for me in my name. We are spending many days in the heat. I have had high blood pressure but now I have it more regulated. There are many problems and preoccupations that I have. Life is extremely expensive. I must work very hard at home. It's in God's hands. The brother of Emilita (my father's mother) died recently, I have been keeping her company. Rafael (Uncle Ralph), my brother, and I talked by phone. He wanted me to call so I called him. He is doing well. Thanks be to God. Mary Christina (my cousin) is expecting, and Frank (my cousin) is getting married again in March. My friends, Lolita, Theresa, and me have kept company with Josefina. Loving thoughts from Lolita. A big hug and kisses from Maty (Matilda) and Mami to the grandchildren.

May 29, 1983

I was very happy when you called on the phone for Mother's Day. I have had extremely high blood pressure. It seems like they have changed their plans, but the motives are the same (the Interest Section?). There are many things to worry about and many problems that I have, so I trust in God that he will help me resolve my problem. Received a letter from Figuito (Uncle Fred my father's brother.) He was checking on how we are doing. He showed a lot of interest for the trip (code for coming to U.S.) we would take. He doesn't know Matilde and I have since December 1978 saved a fee for entrance into the United States. My documents are in the Interest Section (formerly U.S. Embassy) here. Matilde's documents I have. They are in my hand waiting for authorization. ... I, as your mother, have priority to leave as soon as possible but to be with Matilde I must wait (due to her medical/mental health.) I hope to go directly from Havana to Miami. That is the humanitarian parole I wish for. (Humanitarian parole allows those who apply for parole from abroad to enter the United States temporarily for urgent humanitarian reasons, such as to receive medical treatment.) I could come through a third country but as I told you the other day I do not like that idea at all. It's complicated because we would have to stay there for some time. I find myself hopeless. I feel very alone and without my dear Francisco (my dad) despite the years since he died. The years don't pass in vain. We hardly go out because everything is extremely expensive and obtaining transportation for me is difficult. I felt badly not being able to go to Annette's wedding (Marilys' daughter.) Uncle Fred says it turned out wonderful, Hopefully, they will be happily married. Do not worry yourself with things that are not important. Your health is the main thing. Write me and tell me if you receive this letter. May you and Joel receive much love, Matilde and Mami.

July 28, 1983

Maria Rosa, with great joy I received the pretty Mother's Day card that you sent me as well as the photographs. I liked them very much. The children are beautiful... I'm pleased to see them happy. I always ask God to guide the children for the future so that they will become people who do well, who are prepared and who can defend themselves. Tell Jody to study a lot so that he can be like his esteemed dad. To Stephanie who studies so much, that she can make it happy for them (parents.) I see that she is in the picture of the honor program that I had heard about (from me.) I'm looking forward to seeing you, but I don't know what to tell you concerning the trip (from Cuba.) I would like you to work it out with Fernando (a cousin in America) because he is very practical and knowledgeable. He can get together a group (for a boat from Cuba) better than anybody else. His company would be an open window for you. I have a huge problem in that Lola (long time housekeeper who was there when I was a child) has an opportunity to get married to a love of her youth. He is a widower and has a little apartment that's pretty nice. ...With all the years she has spent with us Lola is getting married. She's part of the family and I trust her. It's hard to find somebody like her today that you can trust. The cost (for Lola) is out of the clouds. It's very hard to find someone like Lola as the payments are huge. What you get in return for your money is so small. This is going to get resolved and I am trusting God to help me. Kisses to the children and loving hugs for Joel and you from Maty your sister and your mother who loves you very much and wants to see you happy.

February 3, 1985

My dear daughter, Maria Rosa. I am sending along an article from the newspaper on January 2, 1985. It says that they are authorizing the departure of relatives leaving this country. Because of that I ask that you send me an affidavit as the ones you sent are expired. Matilde received a letter communicating to her the agreement that was made. We are waiting for the affidavits so we can notify the interest section. It seems like everything is going to be solved, God willing. Hopefully, it will be good for everyone. I am looking forward to seeing all of you. To see my beautiful grandchildren and to give them a kiss and great big hug. I am excited about seeing you too. Everybody is impressed with my son-in-law (Joel), so I am extremely excited to meet him. It doesn't seem real that we are going to get to see each other. It's never late when the gain is great (a proverb.) I am hoping that God will help us to realize (our dreams.) Luicita (Aunt Louise) is feeling very wore out. She tells me it is difficult for her to send the medicine for Matilde. This is why I am telling you to try to do it in Miami. There are people who help to send medicine in the mail. The medicine is called Sparine 50 mg (Wyeth.) ... Kisses and the love to all from Maty and Mami

August 5, 1985

My dearest daughter Mara Rosa. I thought it was strange you didn't try to call me on the phone after you talked to my friend, Amalia. The trip can't be taken. At the interview, because of the problem (Schizophrenia) with Maty, the waiver was not considered. You cannot imagine the disgust and problem it caused me. We were so looking forward to a reunion with you and to get to know my grandchildren. But destiny has allowed it to happen this way. Besides being anxious we did not count on any help when we presented medical care as a logical need in 1978. I talked to God. It was on my heart. I asked God if our presence there (in Titusville) was going to cause problems. Would the trip cause problems? I would like to hug you some day. It takes a great effort to cook as I am in a great battle with arthritis in the knees and it hurts very much. I am thankful to Lola who helps me wash the dishes and stands in line at the grocery store for us. I don't know what would have happened to us (without Lola's help.) Kisses from Maty and Mami

August 25, 1985

I find it very strange that I didn't get a letter from you, not even a phone call after communicating to you the difficulty we had with the trip that Maty's case was not considered for a waiver. In fact, everything in life is questionable or luck. So, there are worse cases than Matilde, but God knows what he is doing. Maybe it was better for everyone that the trip turned out that way. I begged with all my heart to our Lord to resolve it the best way. I was very distressed to find that they were not going to give me any help over there (U.S.) It's been seven years since we let people know we wanted to leave. Things have changed. We were given no help in any way over there – not even Medicare. I don't want to be a burden. And so, it looks like based on what's going on we have to accept God's will. We are incredibly sad about it because we were excited about being reunited with our grandchildren. I went for a checkup at the hospital and when they analyzed the x rays, they said it was Diverticulitis of the colon. The doctor guaranteed me it was not something to worry about. I have always had good health. It is clear that the years don't go by in vain. I hope that when things get normalized you can come to see us. Don't lose that hope that you have that we will see you. Kisses to my grandchildren and for you too. Maty and Mami. Tell Stephanie to write me.

September 23, 1985

Dearest daughter Maria Rosa. I received your letter, and I was very surprised that you didn't know that besides the affidavit it was necessary to include a copy of your 1040 and W-2 that the "Section of Interest of the United States of America" requires showing that your husband has paid his income tax for 1984. I don't ask for anything without reason. All people that are going there (U.S.) or are coming here need these affidavits. Explain that to your husband. I can't believe you guys didn't understand this. Well, it is getting very late. Because of all the difficulties with this trip I have decided not to go on the trip. God doesn't want us to go on this trip. I asked him very much to resolve what's the best for all. I was worried a lot that we would get there without the help they used to give. These things are very necessary. With regret of all my soul I had illusions of reuniting will all of you. But without God's you cannot go. I hope that God will let me see you at the earliest opportunity... Love to all. Maty and Mami

This was one of the last letters I received from my mother. During this time, she found a way to send money and jewelry to me in clandestine ways. Other communications from her and family during and after these dates informed me that my mother had sold to her neighbor a replica of a Louis XV couch that came from my maternal grandmother Luisa's house. This neighbor had family in Europe who sent me a substantial amount of money for the couch in the form of a check which I secured in a CD. Also, valuable jewelry was smuggled to me by at least one ambassador coming from Cuba to Miami who had diplomatic immunity. My relatives in Miami acquired the jewelry and my Uncle Ralph brought it to Gainesville where I picked it up. All of this was going to be a way to finance my mother's anticipated relocation to Titusville. When this did not transpire, she told me to use the money for the grandchildren's education.

As I translated these letters for placement into this book, I wept frequently even though they were written 40 years ago. I was reminded of the "Why?" questions. While translating these letters I told myself over and over "I should have done more and maybe it's my fault that she was not able to come." Her crushed dream to unite with me, my husband and my children was heartbreaking. However, she repetitively said "I pray for God's will" echoing the theme of this book, "All things work together for good…"

My mother died the next year (1986) at age 84. A relative contacted me a few days after the day of her death describing the cause of death as a heart attack. My mother was such a strong, God-fearing woman who genuinely loved me and my sister. What a sacrifice my wonderful mother made for both me and my sister, Matilde! Even though I miss her and grieve for her at times, I only have loving, fond memories of her.

After my mother's death I received calls from and called a man who identified himself as a "Catholic priest in training" who was helping my sister. I may have talked to him even before my mother's death. He informed me that he had moved people into the home to help care for Matilde, even a psychologist. I will never know. I had talked with my sister during calls to or from my mother for brief conversations. After my mother's death and during these talks with this gentleman I do not remember talking with Matilde. My sister died a short while later. I believe she was only age 54.

In March 2022, Joel, my youngest son, Zach, and I visited The American Museum of Cuban Diaspora, Miami, Florida. This museum is dedicated to the historical and cultural contribution of the Cuban exile community. At the time of this visit and our reason for visiting was their exhibit "Operation Pedro Pan: The Cuban Children's Exodus." It was very moving for me as I was one of those children

61 years before. One of the most impacting elements of the museum tour were the placards on the walls inscribed with the reflections of those who had been children like me on those Pedro Pan flights. One wrote: "When the plane took off, I knew that my life had changed completely." Another noted" ...The minute the plane took off, my first life came to an end." A comment by another was: "I finally realized what had happened during that day and that I might not ever see my parents again. I started crying that day." A final statement that struck me was: "The world changed while I slept, and much to my surprise, no one had consulted me."

Most of these Pedro Pan children were eventually reunited with their parents and their fears and pains were relieved. As I pondered those exhibits that day in Miami, I realized that the reflections of these Cuban immigrants were prophetic for me. All of these remarks had come true. Now that my Papi, Mami and Matilde were gone, THAT DAY I BOARDED THE AIRPLANE FOR AMERICA IN 1961 WAS THE LAST TIME I EVER SAW MY PARENTS AND SISTER and I was only 11.

Chapter 7 The Return Home

ON MAY 16, 2012, I returned to Havana, Cuba for the first time in 50 years. From my daily journal and transcripts from our family videos of our trip to Cuba I will give you as personal an account of this momentous event as I can including exact quotations. Here we go:

Tuesday May 15th, 2012

Last night we went to our grandchildren's piano recital. Jace (Jody's oldest son) sang and played but I couldn't hear him very well as he was pounding on the keys a little too hard. He has a beautiful voice. Afterward he played the Star Wars theme, and he did great! Judah (Jody's youngest son) did well too but he wasn't ready to sit down. I believe he really wanted a trophy besides his certificate. Savannah didn't get to perform her song from Aladdin since she was home with strep throat. Both Vanna and Caden (Stephanie's daughter and son) were not feeling too well with fever. As a result, I didn't think Stephanie would be able to go with us to Cuba. She was really torn up about it, but the doctor convinced her that it would be alright.

Now we have a scale in the house and my life will never be the same. Joel spent the night weighing our suitcases and distributing our clothing so each suitcase would not be too heavy. Tuesday is here and everything is ready. I was busy watering and feeding my cats and sticking pins in my hair until Joel and Jody hollered at me to leave and off, we went. Joel forgot his GPS, so we had to borrow Tommy's when we picked up Stephanie. I got to kiss my warm grand baby's goodbye. Enroute to Miami I read my Bible, then an article about Camilla Windsor (Prince Charles' wife) and tried to do a crossword puzzle. I talked on the phone to my cousin, Ralph (Rafa) de la Sierra, in Miami and got additional family information in case we get to look for my family's farms in Artemisa, Cuba. He's not sure he will get to meet with us at the airport in Miami as both he and Marta (cousin on the Baro' side) had grandchildren events to attend today. If not, Maybe I can see them in June when there's a small family reunion in Fort Walton Beach, but Marta won't drive so far away... I am beginning to get excited.

Jody made our travel arrangements through a Cuban owned travel agency in Miami. They contracted flights through various airlines and charter airlines. Our departure flight was with Sky King charter flights which was founded by the Sacramento Kings basketball team. Sky King operated out of Miami a fleet of Boeing 737's. Our flight number was #5901 departing at 3:00 pm. Our return flight was with Delta Airlines. It was only a one-hour flight from Miami to Havana and vice versa.

At the Miami airport there were the customary tasks to take care of before departing but this time there were new ones. After weighing our luggage, they weighed each of us to make sure that there was not too much weight on the plane. My daughter and I were not too thrilled with this. Then we had to convert our U.S. currency into Canadian as it had the best conversion rate in Cuba. In Havana we would have to convert Canadian into Cuban currency. However, Cuba has a dual currency system, and we were advised to convert to the Cuban Peso (CUP) and not the convertible Peso (CUC.) "

We had lunch at Café Versailles in the airport terminal which had a scaled down menu from its parent restaurant also in Miami, Versailles Restaurant, the most famous Cuban Restaurant in the world according to many sources. I think most of us had Cuban sandwiches, black beans, and rice and pastelitos. Now we waited." "While awaiting our flight sitting next to Jody, I listened to him talk with Stephanie about the changes taking place in the leadership of missionaries to Central America, both of whom would be present in Havana when we arrived. Joel used his miniature, waterproof, sports camera to record us while

Zach read one of his many Star Wars books. Before I knew it, we began boarding.

Once on-board Jody took the camera and began narrating. He wanted to get my mood and reaction just prior to landing in Havana. He narrated in a similar style to that he had used for many of his 16 years for NASA in Public Affairs at Kennedy Space Center where he was regularly being filmed by the media or was making his own media presentations to the public as the Space Shuttle spokesman:

While standing in the aisle of the airliner Jody announced, "Here we are now, boarding our plane to Havana. This is Mom's first trip home since 1961. Hey mom, Ready to go?" he questioned after directing the camera toward me sitting in an aisle seat. Looking back at him I replied, "I can't believe it. It doesn't seem real." He then wanted to know if I was excited, and I responded in the affirmative noting that it had not hit me yet. I did complain to him that I was not in the window seat where Joel was sitting and said that I was going to sit in his lap. Joel overheard our conversation and offered his window seat to me. We squeezed past each other as I maneuvered myself to the window. Jody joked, "Ah, lookie there. Dad's giving up his seat. Chivalry is not dead. Mom is getting the window. Smart man."

As I looked out the window and then at the passengers on the plane, I noticed that most were Cubans or like my kid's half Cuban. After takeoff I looked pensively out the window and around the plane almost oblivious to what was going on. In almost no time the landscape of Cuba came into view. I just stared at my former homeland. Upon seeing what I saw Jody asked, "Hey, Mom, can you see clearly? I just got a shot out the window (with the camera.) "I resumed peering out the window. I could now see mountain-like terrain. As we neared Havana I began nervously digging at the skin on my hands and then looking where I had just prodded without realizing it. Before I knew it, we were landing at Jose Marti Airport, Havana, Cuba. Next the pilot began to welcome all passengers to Jose Marti airport first in broken English and then in fluent Spanish. Silently I looked out the window with a degree of apprehension while the pilot spoke and the chatter on the plane rose a decibel or two.

After the plane landed and we waited to disembark I began chatting with a Cuban American grandmother who was holding a large blond doll for her granddaughter who she would be visiting. It was ironic that one of my last memories of leaving this same airport 50 years ago, although unpleasant, involved a doll. Upon my departure from the plane, uncharacteristically I rushed down the stairs leading from the airplane to the landing strip. After I touched the tarmac, I immediately knelt on it and kissed it. Jody did not capture it on camera, but Joel saw me. He said he was touched by my actions.

We all walked across the tarmac toward the terminal with me leading the way. I was trying to take it all in as I walked with Zach. It was noisy from the roar of the airplane engine and an airport vehicle that sped past. This was Jody's third trip to Cuba since 2010 and he began answering our questions.

Jody queried, "Alright Mom. You're here. What do you think?" After he hugged me, I smiled and asked him if this part of the terminal was different from when I left 50 years ago. "This is probably a newer building" pointing to another building in the distance he identified as Jose Marti primary airport. Excitedly I revealed, "That is where my parents said goodbye to me!" At this time, we followed Joel into the terminal. We had checkpoints in customs to clear.

I entered a small room with a window opening and a lady in her 40's sitting behind a desk. Standing in front of the counter separating us I handed her my visas and passport. She reviewed them. My picture was then taken. She questioned me about my full name which is "Maria Rosa de San Jose' Baro' y de la Sierra." Her récords read, "Maria Rosa de San Juan Baro' y de la Sierra." In her effort to be efficient she seemed exasperated when I corrected their records. Finally, she agreed to change the name and let me go through the door leading out of the small room.

At last, we found the suitcases and met the President of the Cuban National Church who took our party to a Toyota van we had rented though the travel agency. There we met our driver, Mario (not his real name), who was bilingual. Until we left on Sunday, he was our constant companion and sometimes travel guide from 9:00 am until about 10:00 pm every day. Mario was about Stephanie's age and the best word I can use to describe him is "simpatico." On the 30- minute journey to our hotel I spent much of the time interpreting for Jody and the Cuban pastor as neither was bilingual. We learned bits and pieces of what was happening with the church in Cuba i.e., "the government has given us permission to purchase a bus, but it will cost $47,000." Occasionally, I glanced at the buildings, the homes, and the many people on the streets. My first perception of many of the homes was that they were abandoned and were in much need of repair as they were multicolored due to badly faded and peeling paint. The sidewalks were poorly maintained and only a few of the homes we saw had any landscaping. Occasionally we passed a building which at one time reflected the beauty of Cuban architecture. I observed that some streets were equivalent to the slums you see in some American cities. The dirt had eroded around the sides of many streets. Most of the people we saw were walking although there would be an occasional car that passed by. Most were older cars, some American made and others probably Russian made.

Shortly, our van turned into the circular drive of our hotel, the Avenidas Quinta Hotel located in the upscale Miramar section of Cuba which was the neighborhood I had lived in. It was such a contrast to what we had been viewing enroute to it. It was a luxurious, European owned resort which was only two years old. We exited the van while Mario helped us unload. As we entered the lobby Mario waited there as we checked in. He would be driving us to a church service that evening at Guanabacoa, Cuba for the conference we were to attend.

Upon entering the lobby, we found it to be lovely, spacious, and modern. It had ivory-colored arches and columns, stately pink and white tile floors and a large skylight at the center which reflected upon an ornate lobby pool beneath it. Matching modern couches and chairs throughout the first floor complemented the décor.

After checking in we went to our rooms. Steph and I stayed in one room while Joel, Jody and Zach stayed in another. The rooms were spacious, larger than most American hotel rooms. They were brightly painted and were furnished with many of the amenities you would expect of a 4- or 5-star hotel, i.e., a fully stocked apartment size refrigerator containing soft drinks with Spanish labeling, coffee pots, towels but no washcloths, and telephones in both the bedroom and bathroom. The bathrooms were nice with both a shower and a tub. The thermostat was set at an icy cold temperature, and we couldn't adjust it. Cable TV was available with some familiar sports and news networks and some unfamiliar programing in Spanish. I do not think cable was available to most in the Cuban community as the expense would have been too great for the average worker who makes about $20/month. In the baggage area at the airport, I observed several of the Cuban Americans on our flight had brought TVs to their relatives even though reception would only be local channels. In addition, we did have access to the internet, but it was illegal for Cuban citizens. (Can't let them find out what is going on in the world or how the rest of the world lives.)

We began getting ready for the evening church service at the campground at Guanabacoa. At least two other American ministers joined us in our van including the UPCI Regional Director for Central America. I have since learned that Guanabacoa was the cradle of the Santeria religion in Cuba. This religion is a mixture of Catholicism and Voodoo. During our visit we observed several Santeria priests on the streets dressed in all white. Jody had communicated to us from his previous visits to Havana that the church people had manifest a fear of these Santeria priests.

It was about a thirty-minute drive to the lovely tree laden "campground" at Guanabacoa. After turning off the main highway we had to drive up a narrow, stony, and curved road to the top of a hill where there was a facility for lodging and a small church building. Upon our arrival one of our first tasks was to give one of the Cuban church officials the things we had packed in our luggage for the people, i.e., clothing, pens, pads, toiletries. My understanding was that some of the conference attendees had traveled up to 14 hours by bus as they came from all Cuban provinces. Most of the attendees were ministers and families including some of different faiths. They all stayed on this rustic campground. The church service was in a small building which might hold 100 – 125 people. No vacant seats existed. It only had window openings but no glass windows and one oscillating fan which did not reduce the heat. We never went inside as there was not enough room for us. We sat outside on folding chairs in the open air each night. I translated for my family when the ministers spoke in Spanish. It was hot each night under the stars, but I can only imagine how hot that packed building was inside. The mosquitoes were terrible and shortly after our arrival we began spraying repellant. They were already singing when we arrived and how those Cuban people loved to sing and praise God. They didn't have much in possessions, but they had the Spirit of God and demonstrated it throughout these services.

Wednesday, May 16, 2012

Breakfast at the hotel was amazing! There was a breakfast buffet which few American restaurants or hotels could rival. Normal breakfast staples like eggs, bacon, pancakes, breads, plus Cuban and choux pastries, a variety of fruits, various meats and of course beverages including Cuban coffee (expresso) or Cafecito. Stephanie had a heart pounding experience after too many Cafecito's. There were even black beans and rice if you wanted it early in the day.

We ate breakfast every morning here and perhaps at least one lunch buffet. There were at least three other smaller cafes or restaurants in the hotel where we ate during our stay. This morning, we ate on the expansive terrace outside the buffet. It looked out over a large triple oval swimming pool with two bridges over each end of the center smaller pool. The deck was painted white with an azure, blue bottom. The patio was decorated with stylish white and blue pvc lounge chairs/ tables, a couple of cabanas and a poolside bar. A large uninhabited plot of land could be observed from this vantage point where kids could be seen playing pickup games of baseball in the afternoon. This luxurious hotel was such a contrast from the residential areas we had seen enroute from the airport.

Next to the hotel was St. Joseph's Catholic church whose cross affixed, grey dome towered over the hotel. I attended this church as a child. We went to the church first thing this day and I could hardly wait to get inside. We met the caretaker of the church and for me he unlocked the staircase that led to the large statue of Jesus that overlooked the sanctuary from the third floor. He was more than life size. He was wearing a regal, full length, purple robe trimmed with gold lace. On his head was a crown of thorns and across his hands was a gold chord. On the wall behind him was a depiction of a golden sun with beams radiating out from it. Upon arriving at the statue, I touched the feet of Jesus like I did when I was a little girl. The caretaker told me it was the exact same statue, and I noticed that his feet were worn from the many people who had rubbed them. This was all very emotional to me as it was as if I again was the little 11- year-old Cuban girl before she went to America to live.

While we were in the church I recalled as a little girl seeing "El Caballero de Paris" ("the Gentleman from Paris") marching down the aisle of the church during the service unannounced. Wearing a black cape, he carried in his arms beautiful flowers with which he adorned the aisles. This was a special occurrence for me as a child as this was not a part of the service. This was his personal act of worship as it was not scripted as part of the service. From my husband's internet research, I learned that his true name was Jose' Maria Lopez LLedin. Legends about him abound and it is alleged that he served time in prison where he is said to have "lost his mind." After his release he would wander the streets of Havana being known for his black clothing including a cape, long, unkempt hair and long fingernails. However, due to his kind and gentle nature he became a beloved character (even by children like me) who was seen daily on the streets of Havana for forty years. After spending eight years in a psychiatric hospital, he died there at age 85 in 1985.

After exiting the church, Mario, our driver, drove us around the side of the church. There was a grotto of our Lady of Lourdes which represented the cave in Lourdes, France where Catholic tradition says Mary appeared to Bernadette, a peasant girl, who had a conversation with Mary, the mother of Jesus. High up on the right side and sculpted into the wall of this grotto cave was a life-size statue of Mary. On the lower left, just outside the cave opening was a statue of Bernadette on her knees looking up toward Mary. I remember as a girl when this grotto was first installed outside the church. One more time I walked up the steps to the gate at the mouth of the grotto, and had my picture taken.

Next, we drove to my childhood home where I was living when I left for America. There was an ugly chain link fence around it just like in the picture Jody had taken on his visit two years before. He had never found anyone home. Mario opened the unlocked gate, went up the steps and knocked on the door. I was close behind him. Mario had to return to the car as he left it running. When a lady appeared at the door, I approached her and identified myself as a member of the family who built and previously lived in this residence. Through the doorway

I could see the glass wall of the courtyard of the garden. The house was under repair and this lady was the supervisor of the work. She revealed to me that the owners were not home. as they "come and go." (They likely have a position within the government perhaps an ambassador.)

I asked if we could come in and she said "yes" except for entering the bedrooms. I gave her a hug and turned to my family advising them that we could come in.

At this point Jody began filming our tour of my former home. Utilizing his NASA experience as a narrator of eyewitness events Jody asked me to describe and give a history of what the camera was recording. What follows is some of our dialogue:

Jody asked me to tell the camera where we were. I explained that a construction crew was repairing the house. I noted that the supervisor lives here, and she was going to let us see it. Jody wanted me to make sure she was okay with all of us coming into the house so in Spanish. I asked her and she was okay with it.

I began giving the grand tour which at times included. this lady. I alternated speaking Spanish and English because the lady did not understand English, and my family had limited understanding of Spanish.

First, we came to a wall of mirrors facing the front door. Unsolicited thoughts raced into my mind, "Get out of my house"" but I did not repeat them. As I turned left entering the hallway I pointed out the small bathroom which was still blue just as it was when I was a child. "It is blue. Still the same color," just as you told us Jody remarked.

He then told me to go where I want to go next. Opening a door on the left as we entered the hallway, I exclaimed, "You got to be kidding me! That was my doll's closet! My toy closet." I reached up and turned on a light with the string hanging from the ceiling revealing a storage closet with items for the bathroom, a cooler, a hose, and miscellaneous items. Jody remarked that it smelled like gardenia.

Opening another door on the left of the hallway I suggested that this must be the food pantry. Jody was busy rounding everybody up and missed my comment as he hurried the rest of the party: He directed, "Come on Dad. Where's Stephanie?

Next, we entered a doorway on the right which led to the courtyard inside the house. I narrated, "This is a little courtyard garden." It still had many of the features that were there when I was a girl. There were some small palmetto-like plants, ferns, and other plants in white pebble sand. There was a window-wall through which we could see the foyer after entering the front door. Also, there was a two-panel window which opened from the living room into the courtyard. Pointing to a picture hanger on one of the beams of the open/beam ceiling revealing the sky above, I informed them that we had a little plaque of the virgin Mary up there. I directed their attention to the little pond in which I had kept my turtles. Recalling an unpleasant event I said, "One time the kitty fell through the roof, because...see the roof is open there." See that's a problem Jody because you have little critters..." "...coming in," Jody finished my sentence.

We left the courtyard and entered the kitchen, which was the next room down the hallway. I gestured to the kitchen floor, "This is the kitchen. Look at the granite floors. These are all granite. As Steph entered, I repeated "the kitchen" to which she responded, "Oh...it's held up!" We left the kitchen and headed down the same hallway. "Look! I said, 'servants' quarters!" which is where they stayed when I was a kid. I continued down the hall chatting in Spanish with the work supervisor.

On my right I came to a door which had been the living quarters for our cook. I opened the door and fumbled around in the dark and found the wall switch to turn on the overhead light which revealed a storage room with stacked lawn chairs, dining chairs and a bicycle. Jody asked if it was a garage or storage room. Unintentionally, I responded to Jody's question in Spanish having just spoke to the Cuban lady.

Then I peered to the left and looked around the door which I was still holding with my hand. I was shocked unbelievably by what I saw. I screamed, "Matilde! Oh God, it's Matilde! Are you kidding, it's cuadro (Spanish for a painting)! Are you kidding it's a cuadro!" Sitting on a dresser in this storage room was a large portrait of my sister Matilde when she was about 21. Excitedly I instructed Jody, "Take a picture! That's my sister!" Jody asked, "That's your sister right there?"

Overcome with so much emotion I didn't respond. I just continued talking about the portrait, "I would give anything...I would love to have that! But I don't know..." I was so excited that I couldn't complete my sentences and was so joyful that I walked back into the kitchen and spun around in a circle. Calling from the hallway Jody shouted, "Hey Mom, Mom come in here quick for a video, show the camera...Again I was oblivious to him as I celebrated, "It doesn't get better than this!" Jody called out again, "Tell me what's inside the room. The video camera hasn't seen what's inside the room. The video camera hasn't seen the picture of Matilde." Both of us walked back down the hall and entered the room again. Coaching me, Jody said, "Take us in there (the storage room.)" Moving stuff around in the room Jody and I entered, and he positioned himself to get a good shot of the portrait. He invited me to give some details, "What are we looking at Mom?" Pointing at the picture after trying to calm myself down I explained, "This is a photo or picture of my sister Matilde. Stuttering I continued "She uh...You see the resemblance, I hope. I always thought she was so pretty, because I was a fat little girl and she was always beautiful, So, what do you think smiling at Jody?" He responded, "She was beautiful."

Pleading I told Jody "I would like to take-purchase this – take it home with me." Jody answered, "We'll see. We'll try. We've got the contact information. We'll call the family and see if we can buy it." I told the lady I was so glad the house was in the process of remodeling, and I hoped it was a nice family living there. Then I asked her to please find out if the owner would care if I could acquire the painting. She was so nice and agreed to ask for me. She gave the house phone number suggesting that we call on Friday.

Next, we walked back through the kitchen when I noticed another familiar room. "Look! Look! That's where the laundry was done by a lady from Jamaica!" I began speaking to the supervisor in Spanish again without thinking. Jody reminded me to speak in English.

Gesturing with my hand on the counter, I revealed, "This is where our servants would eat, and I would love to eat with them because for breakfast they would have Cuban bread, and they would have café con leche. Bread and butter were our favorite." I opened the green cabinets above the counter and again began speaking Spanish while smiling to the Cuban supervisor. We exited the laundry room and entered the dining room.

Like a tour guide I enlightened my entourage of family members, "This is the dining room, and we had Nochebuena (Christmas Eve) here. Supper was here most of the time - sometimes lunch too." Jody cautioned me about my speaking in Spanish so much, "Just for a heads up you probably want to speak to us in English. Some of the things you may want to tell us may not be okay (for the staff to hear.) Continuing my tour, I pointed to the end of the dinner table noting, "I used to sit here." Directing their attention to the silverware chest behind my seat, I let them know, "This is where our silverware chest was." I tried to open it, and the lady told me the chest was locked. At this time, I observed a chandelier above the table, sundry glass knick knacks and a mirror on the wall which I didn't recognize.

From here I walked toward a familiar swinging white door with a glass pane for viewing which led into the kitchen. It prompted me to reenact a story I had told about my childhood to the family regarding me and my nanny. "You see this? Look at these. Take my picture!" Grabbing the swinging door and pushing the door stop out of the way I struck a pose. "This is the famous door where my "TaTa" (my nanny) ... Jody finished my sentence, "Oh, looked through the glass."

I began I mimicked my "TaTa" as I peeked through the glass opening with squinting, angry eyes like my nanny. Jody continued his narration, "This is where the nanny looked at her through the door when she was going to tell on her nanny for spanking her." Jody used the camera to create a close up of my eyes behind the glass pane. Zach began to cackle at my gestures. Finishing the story while laughing Jody said, "...and the nanny saw her getting ready to tell her father and mother what was going on and at that very moment the nanny looked through the window at her as if she could read her mind." I came from behind the door and feigning anger at my nanny's behavior I commented, "That was just unbelievable. Perfect timing! Perfect timing!"

As I began walking away the camera alerted Jody that the battery was low. He stated that we could charge it overnight. We moved toward the living room where we came to the bar and gesturing with my hands I announced, "This is the bar. I like that it was hidden away from children. My Daddy had a big apple here," as I pointed to a spot on the bar. "It was an ice cube container. It was red on the outside and silver on the inside to keep it COLD!"

We continued through the living room and outdoors. These are the abbreviated notes of the remainder of my home tour that I journaled later that night. "As I was perusing my former home the same living room and family room furniture were there – they had been re-upholstered, and the couches needed reupholstering. The rattan furniture was there. It didn't look as fresh & gleaming smooth as I remembered it. The furniture in the foyer was not what we had. We had a rose leather couch which was the same one in Matilde's painting. Instead, they now had vinyl coated dark wicker furniture which was more suited to a family room than an elegant foyer. The two large, olive, and white, round Chinese planters were gone. In the family room the rattan glass lunch table & chairs & my little rocker were not there. Not all the wrought iron furniture was in the backyard either. It was white.

There was something where my swing set was in the corner (of the yard) maybe a bench..."

I was able to go to the other side of the house past the large glass & metal doors leading to the hallway and bedrooms. We used to put our large American Christmas tree in front of those doors. I remembered looking at the reflections of the lights - large Christmas ornaments, and the bubbling, dropper-shaped lights from the hallway on the other side. They had locked our bedrooms and the bathrooms on that side of the house. The large chair on the right side of the door to the garage was gone. The green couch was gone but I thought I saw the beautiful dark, antique wood secretary desk."

Before departing my home, we took some family pictures in the foyer of the house with the glass pane wall as a background behind us. I reflected with delight: "No matter what happens, this trip to Cuba has been more than worth it so far and it's not over yet."

Next, we went to Vedado to visit both of my grandparents' homes. *Insight Cuba* a travel blog describes this exclusive neighborhood this way: "One of the best ways to spend a day in Vedado is to simply wander the grid of stunning mansions from this era (after Spanish-American war) each boasting one-of-a-kind Cuban architecture. Nowadays, many of these properties are still single-family-homes, but a remarkable number of them were converted into state offices, government-sponsored cultural centers, and embassies after the 1959 Cuban revolution. Imagine going to work every day in a historic mansion with lofty ceilings and marble staircases." I mused with sarcasm, "Yes, imagine that! Imagine that you are the grandchild, like me, of two of the owners of these properties. You have fond memories of visiting, spending the night, dining, and playing in our elegant homes only to read how the government has been so gracious as to grant the privilege to employees to work in an architecturally exquisite building that they seized and did not work for or build." Sadly, this is what communism does. These thoughts were in the back of my mind as I visited each of my grandparents' mansions in Vedado.

The following narrative is from my daily journal I kept while in Havana: "On this day we also visited my grandmother Emilia's house, my dad's mom. I never met my grandfathers on either side of the family as they had already passed by the time I was born so I only knew these properties as my grandmothers' homes. This home is now the habitation of another governmental agency which hosts educational and cultural groups from around the world. If I gave the name a reader could easily research it on the internet as it is a very prominent institution in Cuba. I won't do that for fear that any family member would be denied travel there if visits are again permitted. Grandma Emilia's home has a half-circle of columns on the end of the massive front porch which made it stand out from other homes in the area. I used to stand at this location and smell the Jasmine. I would serenade anyone who would listen to me sing. My parents would encourage me to sing so I sang love songs in Spanish or songs from the movie *South Pacific*. Until today I did not realize that there was a carriage house for carriages and a driveway on the side of the house for horse-drawn carriages. Horses were kept in an area on the right side at the back of the house where it was walled off. On top of the carriage house is an apartment for my grandmother's housekeeper, Sofia, who was from Veracruz, Mexico. She was nice to me, once making me a beautiful, pink-flowered sewing box from a round cookie tin. Also, she made me a green-and-white cat head made of cloth to store hankies and such. Once when she came back from Mexico, she brought for me boy and girl Mexican dolls in costume. I loved them."

"In grandmother's house the upstairs elevator was broken (yes, she had her own elevator.) I was told by the director of this agency that the upstairs section was added after this house was finished and that it was more modern. I knew this because I had spent the night there many times. Recollections of this home included thinking I heard Santa's sleigh bells while I was supposed to be sleeping, drinking my cereal in a bottle, and falling asleep all dressed up after going to the circus with my parents or Uncle Willy. (I hated sleeping in my clothes!)

"At the main entrance to the house (now government agency) the tile on the front steps is new and red. Originally, they were marble. I learned that a tree had fallen upon them during a hurricane. Inside the building the tile on the dining room walls by the elevator does not match the tile on the floor although it's an attractive brown. It has been replaced from the original as well. I am sure the man in charge who was our guide didn't buy our story about us being interested in Cuban architecture. (We were absolutely interested in this but due to my firsthand experiences at these homes it was much more.) Again, Jody took pictures of us with these employees. We were not allowed to take pictures inside as all the rooms were locked. I was allowed to take two gardenias from Grandma Emily's, and they are now in a glass with water on my nightstand in the hotel as I am writing. I hope to press them in a book, maybe my Havana Social Directory Jody brought back on his first visit to Cuba."

"Next (stop) was Grandma Luisa's home, now the office of another government agency. Knowing only that we were from the U.S. (per previous guidance) they allowed us to go in and look around. Once again, we could not go into the bedrooms which were all locked prompting me to wonder "what is behind those doors?" The employees were welcoming and kind to us. I pointed out to Joel the winding, marble staircase. Just as I did when I was a little girl, I counted the 27 steps to the top of the stairs. Once upstairs we went out onto the terrace from which we could reach the top of a plumeria tree which was full of flowers. The man in charge was so kind as to break off a branch for me. I planned to take and press the flowers in a book. We told the employees of this agency that we wanted to look at the beautiful, old Spanish architecture and admired their remodeling efforts, but Jody took so many pictures of me and the family posing around the house that I am sure they suspected something. A lady employee gave us some good tourist information about the cannon at the fort being fired every night at 9:00 pm which had been a tradition for 200 years. She also claimed that the family who had previously lived in this mansion abandoned it and went to another country, so they (the government) took it."

"I thought to myself, "What nice houses, churches, clubs! What a pretty country and how beautiful is the music! How magnificent are the remodeled cars! How artistic are the people! It's almost paradise! So, why did the owners just walk off and leave this beautiful place? Why would they leave their loved ones or not leave them with other family members?" I wanted to say, "Of course we left. The government took our livelihood, our farms, our rental properties, our money, and our freedom!!"

"I walked around the property for a while like I did in a dream, I once had which made me think of my mother. In my dream I passed her as I walked on the other side of the street and watched her walk up to my grandmother's house. I called out to her, and she looked back but she didn't recognize me. Then I walked up and hugged her. If only that could have been reality and not a dream."

"As I think back it was nice of the director of the agency at my grandmother's house to gather the very fragrant plumeria flowers and give them to me. It was a thoughtful gesture as at that time I was thinking about all my family had lost. He didn't have to be so kind! The loss of this property was not the fault of this man as he just worked there.

Later that day we went to Colon Cemetery, also known as "Necropolis Cristobal Colon, named after Christopher Columbus. It is enormous as over one million people have been buried there since it's construction in the late 1800's. This storied cemetery has become a tourist attraction due to the magnificent and beautifully designed mausoleums within its gates. Upon entering the Romanesque portal to the cemetery Jody spoke with Andres who was a caretaker/guide.

Based upon Jody's research at the cemetery on a previous visit he had determined that my parents and sister were buried in the Quintana (my maternal grandmother's family name) family plot. Andreas told me that there was extra space in this plot since there was no room at the Baro'y Milian family plot of my dad's side. Once inside the gate of the family plot, I laid a gardenia on one of the headstones, the gardenia I obtained from the Calle B house (Grandma Emilia) and the pink plumeria flowers from my Granma Louisa's house. I hugged and kissed the gravestone."

We continued to tour the cemetery after this moving event for me. One of the most magnificent mausoleums was that of Juan Pedro Baro. "Was he a relative about whom I never had heard?" I wondered. There would have been good reason to not talk about him as he had a scandalous affair with Catalina Lasa in the early 20th century I learned from Andreas. This affair led to the first divorce in Cuba and excommunication by the Cuban society. After Catalina died in Paris Juan had her remains brought back to Cuba by boat and it is said that rose petals were thrown into the ocean all the way back to Havana. I peeked through a broken glass in this mausoleum and saw glass panes etched with rose colored flowers.

It was warm, muggy, and drizzly as Mario drove us from the cemetery to a paladares, a small, family run restaurant, with a great ocean view. The house had a beautiful pool which appeared to drop off into the ocean. The Cuban government now allowed such restaurants in individuals homes. Jody bought Mario's lunch. The food was excellent. I ate pargo, which is snapper with their own sauce. It was wonderful! I asked the waiter (the owner) if they had tres leches and he responded that they would have chocolate tres leches tomorrow. This restaurant was a little pricier than the government run restaurant.

I was beginning to get attached to Mario like a son. I thought, I want Mario to get the Holy Ghost! He told me about his wife and family and some of his religious beliefs. There were times when Jody spent time talking with him explaining the services, the animated worship of the people and even the plan of salvation. I pray that someday all of what he experienced that week with our family, the ministers and the church people will lead to him and his family finding the truth.

Wednesday evening, we returned to the Guanabacoa campground. It was the same crowd, and they exhibited the same level of exuberant worship as the previous night. I never detected a decline in the worship, singing or response to the preaching. Neither the heat nor the length of the service had any impact on these precious people.

Thursday, May 17, 2012

Thursday morning, we went to Iglesia de Santa Rita de Casia, which was the Catholic church my mother most attended as it was nearest to our home. I still recall in one service there I forgot to give the offering my parents gave me. Another time I remember sitting on the pew and using my white fan with small red roses painted on it. Another fond memory was the wedding I was in at this church as a young girl. Prior to my mother and sisters anticipated relocation to

America my mother sold some of her household articles at this church circuitously sending the proceeds to me to hold for her. Throughout this trip I was amazed how visits to customary locations in my childhood triggered so many insignificant events when they happened.

There were posters all around the church commemorating Pentecost Sunday which is an annual event within the Catholic church. That celebration that year was celebrated on Sunday, May 27. While at this church we met a couple of ladies who were like caretakers. Pointing to their announcements around the church I took the opportunity to talk about the day of Pentecost in the Bible. I advised them about our "Pentecostal" conference that was moving to a local Baptist church on Friday and Saturday. They showed interest. The next day Mario drove Joel and me back to this church to give the two Cuban ladies the address to the conference location. One of the ladies was there who revealed that she had sustained an insect bite which gave her a fever and necessitated antibiotics. This would prevent her from attending but she said her friend would probably attend. I did not see her during the days I was there but there were many services that I was unable to attend."

Across the street from the church was an outdoor fitness park which also had a soccer field. It was for adults as there were quite a few adults in the park that day. The equipment was not like anything I have seen in the U.S. Jody joined them and experimented with the equipment which proved challenging. The Cuban people are not paid well, and they depend upon the government for subsidies for healthcare, food, and education, etc. They do not have cable TV the internet was not allowed when we visited. As a result, one positive from this that we observed was that the people exercised, walked, played sports, etc. into the evening. What other entertainment could they afford? On his first trip to Cuba, a minister's son who accompanied Jody to his European built hotel, asked to go in as he had never seen the inside of these nicer hotels. Once again, "Don't allow the people to become aware of the lifestyle of the rest of the world!" Afterward we continued our sightseeing driving to the "Copacabana" Hotel. Stephanie jokingly sang "Copacabana" as we toured this landmark made famous by the singer Barry Manilow. The mood in the van changed dramatically as we drove toward the "Old Havana" section of the city. Upon the entire wall of a multi-storied public building was a stenciled image of Che Guevara and alongside this image was an equal size Cuban flag. I have never understood the fascination of anyone with Che who was not Cuban and was a despicable Marxist revolutionary who was responsible for the death of many Cubans. Depictions of Che were prominently displayed in the museum at the Presidential Palace at Revolution Square which was our next destination.

Visiting this area of the city was an unpleasant experience for me and I cautioned Zach as we approached the museum at Revolution

Square. "Walk around like you have been here before and don't say too much. Don't say anything!" We toured the museum which was an exercise in propaganda. Batista was still in power when Castro's troops stormed the palace and overtook the government. While in this building I had my picture taken with some of the bullet holes in the wall from Castro's siege as a background. Zach was a history major in college, so he bought a book from the bookstore which of course was Pro Castro and the revolution. I could not get out of this building quick enough.

Not far away was a Cuban restaurant in an old run-down building sorely in need of repair. On the second floor was a restaurant which served excellent Cuban food. Mario took us there but did not eat with us. The prices were not bad. It was a "government run" restaurant. Our bellies now full, Mario drove us to "Old Havana" which was only a short distance away. As a child I visited this area many times, especially shopping with my mom. We were allowed to purchase tourist items, but we had been instructed to buy only items which were "artistic" in nature. Otherwise, we might not get it through U.S. Customs in Miami when we returned. To say the least we stretched the definition of "art." Old Havana was not a misnomer as the buildings were old and dingy. It manifests some beautiful architecture and painted on the walls of the buildings were life size people from the late 19th Century in the attire of the era. I bought a servant doll among other things and Joel bought a straw hat like what Andy Garcia wore in the movie "For Love or Country: The Arturo Sandoval Story" a true story about a Cuban jazz trumpeter. From that day until today we affectionately refer to Joel's hat as "his Andy Garcia hat."

In a neighboring market area were street vendors, a woman with an amazing voice singing, a woman smoking a Cuban cigar the size of a small ear of corn and even a Santeria priest. Jody had visited this area on his first trip to Cuba in 2010 where he asked a vendor if there were any memento's he could take back to me. After giving the man some background about my heritage, the man said he knew just what he wanted. He produced for Jody three large album like books: *Libro De Oro de la Sociedad Habana* 1949 & 1955 (Roll of Honor of Havana Society 1949 & 1955) and *Directorio Social De La Habana* 1960 (Social Directory of Havana 1960.) To Jody's amazement and later to mine, my name was listed along with my family in the 1955 and 1960 volumes. We have had a lot of fun over the years looking up prominent Cuban Americans in these books. One name we found is Andy Garcia, the actor I previously mentioned. In the "town square" in addition to several stores there was another beautiful Catholic Cathedral, which I believe I had attended as child. Zach questioned me whether we had to go to another Catholic church. We went inside this cathedral on Saturday when we returned and observed a service that was underway.

That night the services continued at Guanabacoa, and we returned to the same location on another hot and humid evening. Refreshing is not a strong enough word to describe their freedom of worship or love for the word of God demonstrated by a people who had so few freedoms and pleasures. This was a place they could experience true freedom and pleasure as God intended, something Americans know little about.

During the day, this same group received teaching including doctrinal issues. The intent of the UPCI was to take advantage of this recently opened window to teach the gospel to the nation of Cuba. As the impact leader to Cuba, Jody was one of those teachers.

Friday, May 18, 2012

Friday morning after breakfast I called the telephone number at "my house" which the supervisor had given to me. I was hoping that she would have a word for me from her employer about Matilde's picture. I became sad and frustrated when a pharmacy answered the phone. I thought how nice it would have been to take "my sister" home. While at the front desk afterward I cried telling the ladies I was enjoying my stay and loved Cuba. I am sure they thought I was crazy.

After breakfast we loaded up in the van and drove to the Friday morning conference service. The services had moved to a sizable Baptist Church in Havana. This was a much larger venue which had many amenities you could find in an older Protestant church in the U.S. Affixed to the inside walls were several oscillating fans which blew onto the audience. In addition, there were louvered windows with openings to allow the outside air to blow into the sanctuary. There was no air conditioning. Hanging from the ceiling were several small chandeliers. A slatted dark wood wall was behind the pulpit and the ministers were seated on the platform which was elevated about two feet above the congregation. The sanctuary was filled with between 300-400 adult Cubans seated in the auditorium. A children's church service was transpiring outside in a courtyard area. Their speaker was a Cuban American minister dressed in a clown suit. Many children were present who were entertained as they roared with laughter at his antics while receiving the word of God.

We had to return to the hotel before the preaching started as Jody had to take one of the ministers to the airport. Joel, Stephanie, Zach, and I walked across the street to the Hotel Melia Habana to eat in one of their restaurants. This hotel was a cut above ours. It had a small running river throughout the large lobby. Tropical plants and trees were strategically located in the seating areas. There were a variety of restaurants within this hotel, and we chose to eat at the Italian restaurant. Joel and I ate cannelloni and spinach-cheese crepes which were excellent. Steph and Zach had lasagna. After lunch we returned to our hotel and hung out until Jody and the ministers returned.

There was going to be a baptism at a beach that was nearby. This proved to be an extremely exciting baptism as it included three pastors of another faith. I wanted to see Mario's reaction. I had to remind myself that this was really what was important, not my picture of

Matilde. It made me happy to be there and I was so glad I went. Jody baptized three men in Jesus Name, and they came out of the water singing and shouting. It was beautiful and I worshipped with them. A lifeguard brought us a bucket of water to wash off the beach sand. One of the ministers attempted to witness to him but the lifeguard said he was a "Mason and did good things for others." The minister responded, "that is a good start but there is more." The sun was setting as this exchange was taking place. Jody joined us and said it was getting late and we needed to leave. He added that he had to preach in the morning.

Upon our return to the hotel, we freshened up and once again went across the street to the Melia to eat a light dinner. I ate a chicken club sandwich, fries and drank lemonade. While waiting I fell asleep at the table which gave my family a laugh. Completing our meal, we returned to our hotel. Before going to sleep I recorded the events of this day in my Cuba trip journal.

Saturday, May 19, 2012

Saturday morning, we had to rush to get to the church as Jody was speaking. There was no clock in the room, so I ran behind. At the breakfast buffet I quickly threw a biscuit, an eggroll and meringue candy in a napkin and put it in my purse. I finished them in the lobby. We returned to the Baptist church.

The Cuban children at the church were beautiful. One little boy with his blond hair sticking up in the front and wearing a white shirt reminded me of my grandson, Caden. Brother Rocca dressed like a clown was doing magic tricks and making animals out of balloons for the kids in the large courtyard. The kids loved it!

During the main service in the sanctuary the songs were beautiful and worshipful, making me cry. "This is probably the last service I will be in," I thought. I wanted to see other places in Havana that I remember but staying for these services was more than worth it. We were unable to attend the service Friday night due to the baptism and

I learned that more than 20 people received the Holy Ghost in that service. One was a man who had never been around church." After the worship service Jody began preaching. What a momentous event for me! My son. My parent's grandson was preaching in the very country they sent me from 50 years earlier to save me from the clutches of an evil despot. Now it had come full circle as my offspring was back in the same county preaching to save Cuban people from the clutches of Satan from whom evil originated.

Jody's text was 2 Corinthians 6:2 – "For he saith, I have heard thee in a time accepted, and in the day of salvation have I succored thee: behold, now is the accepted time; behold, now *is* the day of salvation. Jody used the story of Zacchaeus from Luke 19 as an illustration pointing out that everyone looked down on Zacchaeus. He noted that Jesus saw Zacchaeus' efforts following Him and climbing a tree to see him. "Jesus saw your effort (the congregation) traveling to this conference many miles and many hours, your hours of worshipping, singing, and dancing during service plus the time you spent in prayer the previous day between services crying out to God. Just as God granted Zacchaeus' wishes that day, He will do the same for you by healing you, delivering you, forgiving you and filling you.

The altar service that followed was powerful. It was a blessing and a privilege to be able to pray with Cuban ladies seeking God. My theme of "All things work for good" again manifest itself. My son had just preached an apostolic message to these hungry souls and here I was helping Cubans pray through to an experience with God. Would this have happened if my parents had not sent me to America? An emphatic "NO" is the answer.

Our late lunch after the church service was at the country club at which my family had been members. I believe it may have been my suggestion to go there. The "club" was one of the nicer looking buildings we visited both inside and outside. It featured classic Cuban architecture with a red Spanish tile roof, off-white walls with the eaves, doors and the arches trimmed in a reddish, mauve color. It was situated on a Caribbean beach, and I nostalgically recalled the thatched huts, palm trees, and lounge chairs on the sandy beach I observed.

Inside we found the country club to be comparable to any in the U.S. It was very upscale and one of the nicest restaurants I have ever been in. I was so pleased that it was much like I remembered as a child. Memories came flooding back of me going through a line to get my food and ginger ale to drink. Usually, my family or my mother and I went at the same time of the day and usually on a Sunday. There always seemed to be an older crowd when we went. This day was different as our group was comprised of my family of five and three ministers. There were no other patrons in this large area of the country club. The food was exquisite as I ate lobster, steak, chicken, rice, and a vegetable. Upon finishing my meal, I had to run to the beach outside where I had played and swam so many times as a child. Unfortunately, there water was not nice that day. When Joel came to get me, I was putting my sandals back on. Disappointed, I told him that there were "all kinds of green plants" in the water." At that moment I reflected how I missed my frequent playmate "Raul" causing me to wonder what ever happened to him or my other friends.

After a brief trip back to the hotel to freshen up, we went to the fort – "El Morro," built in the 16th century. This fortress guarded Havana harbor and was situated on an elevation above Havana. I had never been there as a child. While there I reflected upon the fact that individuals during the revolution were imprisoned and likely some died there.

From this vantage point we could view the harbor, the Malecon and the skyline of Havana. We explored the grounds, the cannons and some of the interior areas of the fort where we were allowed. Vendors selling trinkets and memorabilia were set up on the outskirts of the fort and we visited them as well. I spent some time here while Joel videoed our activities. Steph and Zach were together a lot of the time and to no one's surprise Jody struck up a conversation in broken Spanish with four young Cuban boys between the ages of 8 and 10. He tried to find out if they were familiar with the Pentecostal church. It was quite entertaining to watch.

We had to make one last trip to Old Havana again. I wanted to get a straw hat that said "Cuba" like the one Stephanie bought earlier. Steph and Zach had pictures made with the backdrop of the building walls painted with stylishly dressed people from the late 19th century. We went inside the old Catholic cathedral where people were praying. Shocking that we went to another Catholic church, huh? We quickly bought last-minute souvenirs and headed out.

From there we drove through the streets of Havana on our way to the famous Tropicana cabaret nightclub. It reminded me of the times I rode with my dad in his jeep on our way home from one of our farms. As a child I had never been to this legendary nightclub as it featured an adult venue with famous singers, dancers, and entertainers. As we toured the Tropicana, I thought to myself "So this is what it was like when my parents told me they were going to the Tropicana and left me at home." There were many American entertainers who came there during the 50's like Nat King Cole whose picture was posted upon the wall of the museum-like area of this nightclub. Celia Cruz was a famous Cuban singer who performed here and coincidentally a nephew of hers lives just two houses down from our home in Mims. The Tropicana is again a thriving nightclub for Europeans and Canadians primarily. We visited during the late afternoon and had no intentions of eating at the restaurant or seeing the show which opened at 7:00 pm and 10:00 pm respectively.

Sunday, May 20, 2012

Our last day was Sunday, and we took pictures outside the hotel with our new friends Mario and the ministers and missionaries that remained. I was sad but I was proud that one of my sons had been and was still preaching in Cuba to the Cuban people, my people. Being able to translate for him as he interacted with those who did not speak English was exciting. It was a blessing to me to be able to mingle with the Cuban church members who had been so welcoming and kind. I just wished we had more time there. My only true regret was that I had not been able to obtain the portrait of my sister, Matilde, and take her home with me. My family and I loaded up in the van and Mario drove us to the airport.

This is a portion of the conversation that we had on the way back to the airport with Mario. As Jody spoke, I translated into Spanish: "We're giving this Bible to you. This section I am holding Acts is the only part of the Bible that gives an eyewitness account of people receiving salvation. The books that follow are written to people already in the church 30 years later. There are many Christians that are not comfortable with this book. But it is in their Bible – it's in every Bible but because of power ... but because they lose power because the leaders will lose control of their church, they tend to read it quickly. The rest of the books Romans, Corinthians, Ephesians, Galatians – all these back here (Jody showing to Mario the books after Acts) are excellent books written by the Apostles for mature Christians to become stronger... They tell how to do great works for God, but they do not give examples of people being saved. They are excellent books written from the apostles to mature Christians, but the only examples of salvation are in the book of Acts. So, I have taken a highlighter and marked all the pages where someone received salvation." (About this time, we arrived at the airport and Jody concluded by telling him) "We hope to see you very soon." Translating like this seems insignificant and unimportant to me, but my husband constantly reminds me that I am invaluable as a conduit for the Lord to deliver the message of the man of God to someone like Mario. Romans 10:14 says, "...And how shall they hear without a preacher."

Not to overstate my position, but I become the "preacher" for these individuals. On this trip I became the "preacher" for my family as they would never have understood the Spanish services. I love and pray for Mario. We became close. I hope to see him in heaven.

A visit to my childhood home with my family 50 years after I left Havana, Cuba.

Grandmother Louisa's Home   Placing flowers on my parents & sisters graves   Grandmother Emilia's Home

Chapter 8 The Miracle of Why?

AFTER WE RETURNED FROM Cuba, we were all pumped about our trip and told anybody who would listen about it both inside and outside the church. It wasn't long before Jody had to start planning another trip to Cuba for 2013 which had surprising new wrinkles. This is the account he gave for the book about this momentous trip to Cuba not only for the church there but for me as well:

"I was in the process of trying to raise money to develop Bible training, ministry training, and conferences in Cuba. You must do conferences in Cuba as a three-day or four-day conference. You can't just do Bible college the way we currently do it with a residential facility with people coming and staying there, getting a part time job, or just working on the campus. You must do your training and your teaching of leaders and pastors and ministers in clusters. So, you do 2, 3, 4, 5 terms a year just to try to cover the content of doctrine and ministry training and so forth. It's very costly because in Cuba you must reserve a facility, you must pay for that facility, and it must be a facility that has the ability to cook and provide food for a period of three to four days maybe five days. It must have places for the people to sleep. Because the people travel from across the island, some of them travel for two days just to get to the location, so you must have all that set up, reserved, and paid for. You must buy the food in advance. There's no "Hey, we're going to take a lunch break and go run to a restaurant!" You can't do that! It must be a self-contained thing just to have a conference. I think back at that time (2013) we were estimating the cost of a conference to be about $15,000, so you can imagine doing three or four of those a year you're looking at as much as $60,000. I had to raise funds for that so you try to make phone calls, write letters, and send emails to pastors that have a heart for missions and those who may have a specific burden for the nation of Cuba.

Having done these before I was writing another letter (for support.) The agenda was to just bring in the typical global missions' content and try to pack it into three or four days. Teaching is in the morning and afternoon with preaching services at night. Then you repeat it the next day. I was putting that agenda together and had estimated what the cost would be. I was writing a letter to go out to all these pastors and right in the middle of writing this letter I got a phone call. I didn't recognize the number, so I let it ring through as I was busy. There was a second call from this number, and I think there may have even been a third call. The third time I answered the call and learned it was Brian Michaels, one of the regional directors for Purpose Institute in North America and, of course, Purpose Institute has a curriculum-based training and teaching format. They run it like a college with college level courses which are incrementally and progressively more difficult and more in depth as you advance through your different terms. Purpose Institute is built with the mindset of people that are not able to go and stay at a Bible college. They realize people must work their jobs and they must live their lives, but they are able to set aside a week or a weekend to focus on teaching and training.

So, I got a phone call from this brother. He started with, "Hey, I understand that you're the contact that we need to make for getting into Cuba." I responded, "Well I'm a fundraiser and I'm a minister that goes there. We certainly are involved with the training and equipping of pastors and preachers in Cuba, but I don't have authority to decide whether we can use Purpose Institute or not." He inquired, "but what are y'all currently doing?" I explained what I said a few moments ago (to the reader.) He said, "What if I told you that we want to launch a Purpose Institute in Cuba and that we're willing to come there and hold classes throughout a week. We cover the curriculum. We're structured for that, doing it all at one time with concentrated content.

We will do that, and we'll come back term after term after term until people have matriculated through a process that would earn them a Purpose Institute certificate of completion. It could take three or four years depending on the scheduling, but we'd like to get started. We'd like to be in Cuba! I said, "I'd love to do it, and I've taught Purpose Institute classes in America. I don't know how it would work in Cuba. They're very restrictive there. I just must be honest with you because it's funny that you're calling me right now. I'm writing a letter to raise money for a seminar the way we've been doing it. What will be the cost for us to do a Purpose Institute? It costs us about $15,000 to pull one of these things off for a weekend. How much would it cost for Purpose Institute? He responded, "I don't think you understand, Brother Wells. We pay for it! Shocked I asked, "What do you mean you pay for it?" He said, "We pay for everything!" I said, "You'll pay for the facility?" "Yep!" You pay for the feeding of the students?" "Yep!" "You'll pay for the accommodations and staying in barracks or dormitories? "Yep!" "Wow! Absolutely I'm interested!" I offered. He said, "Well let's talk. I want to put you in contact with Brother Ellis." I reminded him, "Hold on a second, I don't have the authority to make that decision. The regional director is Brother David Schwarz, and he has the authority. He can speak to the folks that run the other program typically used for Bible College programs for the global missions' fields. He will get us an answer. Who should we have them (Global Missions) call? He answered, "why don't you let me know and I'll call them and work it out."

So, we went through all those details and jumped through all those hoops. Global Missions regional director Swartz was immediately open to it. Swartz ran it up the flagpole at headquarters, came back and said "Let's do it. We're ready to do it."

From there it was my responsibility to book the trip and to start putting the travel plans together. Who was going on the trip, who was coming to launch the first Purpose Institute term? Who were the teachers going to be? What were the topics and sessions provided by Purpose Institute? I was told that when they went to a new field of labor Bishop Joe Ellis, who was the president of Purpose Institute, always went to establish an Apostolic anointing there and to kick it off as a new ministry. Brother Ellis was more than welcome to come. Having completed my invitations our entourage would include Brother David Schwarz, Brother Joe Ellis, Brother Mark Hattabaugh, Brother Hector Maldonado, Brother Scott Guinn, and myself. Brother Guinn was a veteran missionary out of Mexico who was going to be coming to visit the Cuban field for the first time and afterward has become highly active there. There were others that came and supported but those were the primary ministers that came. Our purpose on this mission trip was to introduce Purpose Institute to the Cuban church, to get the pastors, the leaders, and their support ministry team members trained. Training in Apostolic doctrine, Apostolic principles, Apostolic structure, and Apostolic governance from a biblical perspective. and we were able to pull it off.

We made the trip to Cuba in May 2013 and once again held the services at Guanabacoa, about 30 minutes outside of Havana. It's teaching, teaching, teaching during the day and then at night you're preaching. However, we always try to have a little bit of a gap in the afternoon to rest, to go back to the hotel, to shower, to change and get ready for the evening service. Sometimes based on the schedule of the teaching, you might get a day to go sightseeing or go somewhere. For me every time I had gone to Cuba since 2010, I had always visited the properties that that belonged to my mom's family. This time I had information about Artemisa, my mom's family-owned farms.

I was responsible for the logistics of the trip and had to plan the transportation on the ground. We needed a bus or large van because we had a larger group this time. It wasn't going to work with a small sedan. At that time in Cuba the moment you bumped up to a certain level of transportation for the larger, air-conditioned bus they require you to have a tour guide. The rules are always changing so I can't tell you if it is that way now. Every Cuban tour guide is going to be connected to the government and so we had a young lady assigned to us. She was devoted and dedicated to us the entire trip. We did not have a different guide, but we did have different drivers. We never lost her. She came with us to a couple of services, and she came with us to all our stops and our visitations and back to the hotel. There were times that she and the driver would run off and do other business while we were set for several hours and then come back and pick us up. I can't remember exactly how that worked out, but I do remember that she was with us a lot. She began to learn my story and found out that I wasn't just an American visiting Cuba but that I was an American whose mother was born and raised in Cuba. I was someone who wasn't just there to scratch a mission "itch." I was someone who loved the Cuban people and had a heritage there. I wanted to be a blessing to them with no strings attached. She began to connect with me. She was very respectful and kind and polite to everybody on the trip, but she was better able to relate to me. Obviously, some of that had to do with the fact that I took care of logistics and oversaw transportation schedules, pick up - drop off, what time and where we were going next and all that stuff.

When I found out we were going to have a gap of time I wanted to investigate pictures of some legal documents (deeds) of family property our family had owned which Mom had provided to me prior to my leaving for Cuba. The properties were located throughout the Havana and Artemisa area. I think there may have been as many as 16 of them. I believe some of them were sugar cane, some of them were banana and some might have been tobacco. I think one was just a literal farm with livestock. I wanted to see these places. I had the time. I had the addresses, and I had a guide. To the driver and guide I inquired if they would be willing to haul us out there and they did. I was able to bring a couple of our mission trip people with us. Brother Swartz was with us on one or two occasions. I think Hattabaugh was with me every time and I think Scott Guinn was with us on a couple of occasions. Since he was with his wife and was also there as a missionary getting a lay of the land of Cuba, he had a mission of his own. Besides teaching, preaching, attending the Purpose Institute conference, and traveling with us he was also becoming familiar with Cuba because he was going to be doing missions work there. However, he was with us on a couple of the excursions.

At one point we were in downtown Artemisa, a nearby city to Havana and I had my iPad out to video and take pictures. I was saying stuff like, "Well Mom I'm in Artemisa" and I was just doing a panoramic turn of the iPad to get video of it. As I panned across, I was standing in front of an old Catholic Church and I thought, "maybe you guys (Mom's family) visited here" on vacations and you went to church while you were on vacation. I panned to the right and there was a big structure right across from me perpendicular to the Chapel or the Catholic Church. The sign on the building said something like "Casa de la Sierra." I thought "wait a second, that's my grandmother's maiden name - my mom's mom" and I shot video of it. There was like a transportation hub of some kind across the street from the hotel and I just shot the video of that too. This transportation group offered taxi driving shuttles, limousine rides, rentals, etc. Perhaps our family had connections to this building right there in the hub of Artemisa, in the downtown area, which is an interesting and very pretty area. In a book by my mom's first cousin, Rafael de la Sierra, he recorded that her mother's side of the family "controlled a great deal of urban real estate and farms" and that my mom's "great-grandfather, "the Golden Ox," made his fortune trading horses to the stagecoaches that traveled from one town to another in Cuba."

I didn't know all this until I got home, and Mom verified it. At the time I thought it was connected or the names were just the same. We went to farms. I shot video and photos of all those places. It was just mind-blowing that all the stories that Mom had told me as a little kid were true. We really didn't have any concept of wealth. We were a middle income, family. We never wanted for anything, but we weren't wealthy. When you hear about families that have butlers and maids and live-in housekeepers and nannies and farms and places that they visit for the summer and places they visit in the spring, none of that stuff had any point of reference for me. It didn't seem like reality and in the back of your mind you're saying, "Mom, are you sure that's the way it was? Do you really remember that was the way it was because we tend to remember things in our childhood as being much bigger than they were? But it was as she indicated. The farms were amazing. The properties were vast. I didn't even get to visit all of them. I didn't have time so I couldn't visit all of them.

Of course, while this is going on my tour guide is realizing not only is this the son of a Cuban exile but one whose family had means. You know he's from a wealthy family - a well-off family which of course is persona non grata in a communist government. Therefore, I was trying to be careful not to draw a bullseye on myself or my family name because I wanted to bring Mom back to Cuba. I didn't want to create any stress for her. I realized that we were getting a little bit too much attention by going to these places, but it was too late at this point. I was so into the research and into finding all this out that it was an adventure.

Next our entourage wanted to see my grandparents and great-grandparents' homes in Havana proper. My great-grandparents' homes are in Vedado, and my grandparent's home (Mom's Mom and Dad's home) was in Miramar. These neighborhoods are close to each other.

They're just a few streets apart and they are both very well-off communities or used to be. Nothing is well off in Cuba anymore, but these were very well-off communities in the glory days of Havana. They wanted to see the houses, so I had the tour guides drive us by there and we went to visit both sides of my mom's grandparents, my great grandparents' homes in Vedado, both of which are now government buildings housing different government agencies. It's amazing. We would call them mansions in America. It was staggering viewing those homes with imported Spanish tile on an outdoor porch or lanai that wrapped completely around the house, not just a front porch, but an entire wrap around with imported Spanish tile. Doors made of solid wood mahogany - 12-foot-high doors. It might be a closet door but it's 12-foot solid mahogany wood. The beautiful architecture was an ornamental very European, Spanish, architecture. They were beautiful, just beautiful homes.

So, we went to the great-grandparents' homes first and then we went to my mom's home in Miramar. My Mom had done research since I had taken her to Cuba in 2012 when she had visited. She contacted our driver on that trip, and she had found out the name of the people that lived in her childhood home and who they were in terms of the Cuban government, so we had a name, a little bit more information. On that 2012 trip we met a caretaker and so it was remarkably interesting to go back there.

The tour guide helped me make a phone call to what we would call an estate manager - someone that manages the property for the owner. The owner of the home is a government official and so he travels a lot. Never met him and still haven't met him but his estate manager would come back and forth from the property as he required. I was able to call on one night when we had a free evening and was able to speak with the estate manager. I asked if we could meet at the property to look and get a hold of the painting my mom found of her sister, Matilda, in her childhood home on the tour that we did the previous year.

I was shocked at how accommodating this estate manager was. She agreed to meet us at my mom's house at about 9:00 o'clock that night. It was after hours. It was later in the evening than we really wanted to be out on the street. But we (Brother Maldonado, Brother Hattabaugh, and myself) loaded up in a cab and drove to my mom's childhood home. When we got there the estate manager was outside waiting for us. She showed us into the house and right there in the front room up against the couch was the framed piece of art, the painting of my Aunt Matilde whom I never met. I was like, "This can't be this easy! There's no way that this is happening!"

I was shocked at how amenable she was. I was thanking her while Hattabaugh and Maldonado were just blown away by the whole thing. I asked if she had any recommendations on how to handle this - getting it out of the country. She responded that's the problem I would have. She said you don't have a problem getting it from us. The current homeowner is more than glad to let you have it. It belongs to your family. But getting it out of the country is going to be difficult because it was painted in 1957 and therefore it is an antique. That's something that must pass the government scrutiny before it can leave the country.

I think it was this lady who said that she knew my mom's mother and sister. I seem to recall that there was a season when grandmother and Matilda were co-occupying the house with the government official. Somebody in the Cuban government was living in the house with them to give care or assistance to them. (My mother later informed me that she had telephone communication with a "a former priest" who brought people into the house including a "psychologist" for Matilde after her mother died.) The estate manager was familiar with them, which I had not known. That was shocking - to meet people that met and knew my family. However, I was overtaken by obtaining the painting. I became very singular minded as I thought "My first objective is, to get this painting out of this house while being thankful. My second objective is to secure the painting to make sure that I can get it home safely to my mother."

After advising she didn't have an answer to my question, she offered, "wish we could help." An implication was that "it's a risk." Another suggestion was that "if you'd rather that we hold on to it, then you and your mom and your family whenever you visit can come see it then. We'd be glad to do that." "Absolutely not, I will take the risk," I responded.

After we returned to the hotel late in the evening my wheels were turning: "How can I get this painting out of Cuba?" My first thought was to try to have it wrapped up professionally looking so that customs personnel won't tear it open. I thought that people will not bother it if you can make it look professionally wrapped. I believed I could make it look official then maybe we could secure it. Also, I didn't want it to get damaged on the flight.

What I did with the help of Brother Maldonado or Brother Hattabaugh or both, I can't remember, was to go down to the back of the hotel to the loading and unloading dock for the restaurant. All the produce and food shipments would come in there so there were cardboard boxes laying everywhere. I was looking for a cardboard box that might fit around the painting. I felt that if I could just find something that was a perfect cardboard box and seal it up in that box, they would leave it alone and not ask any questions. I should be able to carry it on the plane I thought. However, I couldn't find any boxes that fit it. I lingered around their pile of boxes so long that somebody saw me on a camera, and they came out. One of the workers inquired if they could help me with something. I said "Oh, I'm just looking for a cardboard box to pack some things in." "What are you looking to do?" they queried. Everything is always questions. They never accept an answer to a question. There must be more questions.

Finally, I found corners that I could put on each corner of the wood frame to protect it from jarring and to provide a little bit of a buffer. So, I had those four corners together and I had pictured in my mind how I was going to make this work. I was getting ready to walk out when the manager of the department in shipping/receiving came out and asked me to step into his office. They brought us into an office and asked us 20 questions. I have no doubt that they were reporting it to some government agency. After answering their questions, they let us go and we went back upstairs.

Once there I got a completely clean, black garbage bag and I took it up to my hotel room. Once there I secured my door. I was hesitant to leave the painting at any point, but I went downstairs to the concierge desk where they had safes where you could secure your private items. I asked them if they had any labeling like a card that has information on it that the hotel signs as private property with their logo on it. The employee said that they did and retrieved a card that recognized a package as a gift. I thought "that's perfect" so I had them fill that form out. It had their stamp and their logo on it. I took that and I laid the painting frame with the cardboard pieces on it, and I secured it with tape that they gave me. I tried to make it look like it just came from a shipping/receiving company - like it was professionally wrapped. The message I was trying to communicate was: "Don't mess with this! Don't break the seal!" and I cut a hole where that gift card or patch was visible so any information you need to know is right here. You don't need to open it up any further. I had sealed it as good as I could.

The next day we were flying out, so we went to the airport. Of course, at the airport you must check in for your flight and you must let them know if there's any baggage being checked, and do you have to declare anything that you've purchased or bought. I showed the bag that I was going to check and the bag I was going to carry on. The attendant inquired about the package, and I said, "That's going with me." "What is it?' she asked, and I said "Oh it's a piece of art." "OK, have you got the receipt for it that shows your proof of purchase" she continued. I countered, "Oh I didn't purchase it. It was given to me as a gift." "How nice, who gave it to you? she probed further. Now, I'm getting into 20 questions again, this time at the airport. I told her that it was given by a family friend and I'm just taking it home. "Well, we'll have to have it looked at of course when you go through customs. "Well, it's all sealed up and packaged for the flight," I told her. "Yes, but we'll have to look at it," she persisted. I was getting frustrated, and they called somebody from what I assumed was customs to meet me in an area to which they directed me. Brother Hattabaugh, Brother Maldonado, and Brother Ellis were walking with me, and they noticed that I was getting a little agitated with this process as I was worried that these officials were going to confiscate this painting from me without me being able to get it home. These brethren began telling me, "It's okay Brother Wells. Just relax. Everything will be fine. We'll just walk through this and talk through this." When we got to the directed location a lady asked me to open the package. I opened the package up and she looked at it. Her reaction was like "Wow, what a beautiful piece of art" and then she viewed at the bottom that it was dated 1957. "Oh, this is a piece of human history, and this has to be approved by our department of antiquities before it can leave the country," she said. Then she suggested that they would take it to the department of antiquities and after a review it would be available for me by next week. I said," I'm leaving today. It needs to leave with me today!"

Now, I'm starting to get a little bit more unsettled because it looks increasingly like I may not get this painting off the island. At this point, the ministers pulled me aside and speaking to the lady in Spanish they say, "Please excuse us for just a minute." They said, "Brother Wells you have to remember that you are not in America we've got to be very respectful." I think it was Brother Hattabaugh who said, "Let's pray!" So, he gathered up with everybody and began to lead in prayer asking for God's hand to be upon the painting and for the Lord to help us get it back to my mom. When we finished praying, I felt peace about it, but I still didn't have any answers as to how we were going to solve this problem.

They were being firm about the situation, so we went back over to the lady. Appealing to her I said, "Ma'am this is a family heirloom, and it's owned by my family. It's not owned by this nation. I just want to bring it home to my mom." Brother Hattabaugh began to talk to her and to explain to her in Spanish that I was half Cuban, and my mother was born and raised in Cuba. He told her they sent her away to live in America and she never saw her family again. She never saw her parents again. They all passed away here in Cuba. He pointed out that the picture was my mother's sister who passed away in Cuba. "This is all she has left." Brother Hattabaugh appealed to her sense of compassion for our family and for my mom. Then he said pointing to me, "He is half Cuban" and she said, "I know! I know!" Then he said, "but the half of him that's Cuban is the half where his heart lives!" At this the lady teared up, started crying, and she started wiping her eyes. I was listening and watching this whole thing as Hattabaugh's sincerity was both heartfelt and amusing. I remembered from traveling in missions' fields that sometimes you can pull out a $20 bill and you can help the process along. So, I reached into my wallet and grabbed a I think a $20 American bill. I started to extend it to her, and she pushed it away from me. She said, "No! No! I will not! I'm not doing this for money!" Apologizing I said, "I'm sorry. I didn't mean any offense by that." She said, "I will do this for your mother! I will do this for your family!"

Relieved I now felt like "Okay we're good! We're done!" Then we had to go through immigration and load up on our plane. We were standing in line to board the plane, all our travelling party together, and Brother Guinn was asking questions about my family history. I began answering and telling these things. Familiar with the history, Brother Schwarz chimed in as well. We were going back and forth, and I wasn't paying attention but a couple in front of us had been listening to our conversation. I was carrying the painting with me and right before we got on the plane the man in front of us looked back and said, "This is my card. I'm a reporter. I'm a writer, a journalist for such and such a magazine. This is one of the most interesting stories I've ever heard. You really need to have this story told. I would be honored to be able to tell this story."

At that time, I didn't believe we needed to have a story that's published in the news media in America about our name, about our estates, about our farms, about our history, about this painting, about what we went through at the airport. We were trying to operate under the radar screen and just minister to people in Cuba with liberty. This would put a spotlight on what we were doing in Cuba, ministry wise. I said I really appreciate your interest but no we can't do that. The man was visibly moved by the story.

As we were boarding the plane the flight attendant asked me to hand her the portrait. I said, "No ma'am this is coming with me on the flight. Defiantly she responded, "No, Sir, it's going into luggage." I said, "This is not going into luggage!" Customs has already approved it. They released it!" She said, "That's leaving the country! That's Cuba's responsibility. This airplane is my responsibility! This battle of wits continued as she started trying to be verbally forceful and decisive. "I'm going to take it and put it under in storage!" she continued. I contended, "Ma'am there must be a way that we could find a place to store this up here. This is a family heirloom. I don't want it to be damaged. It's very fragile and I want it to make it home to my mom.

Once I got it on board I inquired if there was a spare aisle seat to which I could belt it right next to me. I told her I don't want it to leave my sight, and she said I can't allow that to be on the seat. I was just being insistent, and she was being insistent about policy. While this verbal battle was ongoing Brother Schwarz had already boarded the plane and found these compartments that they have on all commercial aircraft. They look like a tiny little door, and you open it up and there's a slot where you might hang a flight attendant's suit coat. It's about a 2 inch by 3-foot door. It's tiny and has a little hinge on it. You open it up and it's just wide enough.

Brother Swartz found one after stating that he thought there's one of these onboard. He asked the attendant if it would fit in there and we walked to the back of the plane. The attendant opened it up and it was like this compartment was custom built for this portrait. It was that perfect of a fit and we just slid the painting into that slot, closed the tiny little door and flew home with it.

We flew back to Miami and got through US customs without a hitch. Obviously, I declared it. I didn't purchase it so there was no financial exchange. We got it home in time for Mother's Day.

Regarding the portrait, it was an interesting experience, incredibly unique. I haven't encountered anything like it, before or after. The feeling was like you were participating in some kind of clandestine operation. Not trying to make it grandiose, but you are in a very controlled environment- a very risky situation. You don't have a great chance of success, and you've got several obstacles to get through to accomplish this. There was a real likelihood of the painting being confiscated and us never seeing it again. You are risking being able to keep it in a safe place of your own determination versus it being appropriated by the hotel, by the airport, by the antiquity's office or whomever. Anybody could take it and keep it. That's just the way things happen there, so it was risky. I realized that this was an all or nothing situation despite being overwhelmed by the commitment required. I either got it home to my mom in person or why have it? It would be meaningless. It either is with my mom or it has no value. Normally, I don't deal with anything the way this event transpired as I always look at this type of matter progressively. I always have a plan - a Plan B or plan C. This time there was no alternate plan and for the purpose to be that singular it was unique for me. Secondly some of this activity was all happening at night, even late at night. This added the stressor of being observed, being watched, or being stopped.

I don't want to exaggerate this event or make it comparable to some other more significant event, but I will. I wondered growing up what it was really like after hearing the stories about the Jews being persecuted in Poland, being rounded up and taken to the ghettos and moved into the ghettos. These persecuted people tried to gather as many of their belongings as they could and would hide their family jewelry, their books, musical instruments, and china. At one time I looked at that and thought how materialistic you are to want to keep all these things. Why should these things matter to you? They are just things! Grab your family and get out of there so the Nazis don't kill you! It seems extraneous but I had a similar feeling of "Wait a second now this is part of the family! This isn't about selling something that has a financial value! It has intrinsic value! It is a part of my family! It represents family members my mother did not get to see after she was a child! It caused me to reconsider my past thinking. I now realize that I wasn't as harsh in this thinking now that I found myself willing to be stopped and my property searched by customs in Cuba. The same applied on the plane and by U.S. Customs when I arrived in Miami. My mindset was, "Whatever it takes to get this there I'm willing to do it!" I wasn't being materialistic at all. There was no desire to make any money off it. This is valuable to my mother, so I'll do whatever it takes to get it to her. I gained a unique perspective on why people might hang on to certain heirlooms because certain things represent something so intrinsically valuable to your family that you are willing to take substantial risks. (There was an Academy Award winning movie in 2015, *The Woman in Gold*, with a similar plot to my mom's. A Jewish woman, named Maria, tries to claim a portrait of her beloved aunt 60 years after she fled Austria. Because it was a national treasure, she only acquired it after great hardship.)

The day after my return from Cuba was Mother's Day 2013. It was funny because I had now been to Cuba four times, and I always had photos and videos when I came back. So, my family was used to seeing these. By this point my dad, sister, Stephanie and younger brother, Zachary were not into seeing these videos and photos, but Mom was. I had asked everybody to come over to my house for Mother's Day so we could give Mom her gifts. Without giving away that I had Matilde's portrait I said there were some pictures I wanted everybody to see and one picture in particular. I began flipping through my iPad going through pictures and I said "Oh, yeah I have one more." I had taken the painting and covered it with a black cloth and leaned it up against the entertainment center in the living room right across from where we were sitting. I said Mom there's one more picture that you need to see. I got up and I walked over to the portrait and pulled that black cover off the painting. Mom was now looking at the painting of her sister that one year ago she had discovered in her childhood home and exclaimed, "I want that painting! That needs to come home with me!" At that time, I promised her I would get it and bring it to her.

Mom yelled "Matilda!" loudly and eventually said "You finally made it to America!" So, it was an incredibly special Mother's Day. My sister was happy and emotional and thought it was a beautiful thing. She was extremely excited to have it. Steph had her picture taken along with Mom and Matilda in my living room.

I may have shown the painting via FaceTime or Skype from the hotel room to Stephanie while I was still in Cuba the night before we flew home. Stephanie couldn't believe it. She just couldn't believe that we were taking it home. Then she became a typical little sister and complained, "Well what in the world am I supposed to get Mom for Mother's Day? She expressed her feelings that what she or Zachary gave Mom could not compete. That wasn't my goal, but I didn't mind it either. It was the best Mother's Day gift she got that day. So, Stephanie used her sense of humor by drawing a small picture of the painting, framed it and made a cartoon looking thing. After I gave Mom the painting she said, "Look Mom, I got you something too." We have had many laughs about that picture which Mom still has on a shelf.

(Jody's account of acquiring Matilde's portrait ends.)

You can only imagine what a magnificent Mother's Day this was for me. At church that Sunday morning, Jody always honors me and my daughter-in-law, Christie, during the Mother's Day service. I was so hopeful that he would have somehow been able to get the picture and would present it to me in church. No, he only had flowers for me that morning, not that flowers are bad. I just was expecting something better than flowers.

After church all the family went out to lunch for Mother's Day. Again, no portrait of Matilde. Now I was convinced that he had not been able to obtain the portrait. When he asked us to come over to see the pictures and videos he had taken in Cuba, I wanted to see them especially since they were of the farms and property my family owned. Maybe I would recognize something familiar, I thought. I must add that Jody did an excellent job of concealing Matilde from me to enhance her portrait's revealing.

A few days after I received Matilde's painting, I wrote to the government official at my former home thanking him and telling him how grateful I was. He responded back to me some time later telling me he was happy to do it. He added that he had some more family heirlooms he would like to give me. Someday that will happen.

The other day my husband and I were walking in our rural neighborhood in Mims. On this day I asked my husband half seriously, "Can I go to heaven for hating Castro due to the pain and heartache he caused in my life?" I knew what he would answer before he responded, "You have to forgive him whether you like him or not." Joel added, "You can almost thank him for what he did, because God uses pain and trauma for good. Look at the life you have had and now have." What would your life have been like if you never left Cuba? Remember your favorite scripture?" Immediately I responded, "...all things work together for good to them that love God..." Rom. 8:28.

I reflected aloud, "yeah, I probably would have married some macho, overweight Cuban guy and would never have had an Apostolic experience and experienced the freedoms I enjoy in America today although they are now slipping away from us. Sometimes, I want to get up on my soapbox like most Cuban Americans and scream to America; "Don't you see what is happening? At a painful personal expense to themselves, my parents gave me to God and America so I could experience true freedom which unfortunately today is eroding and headed in the opposite direction. Holding a similar sentiment is my college age, Chinese-born granddaughter. Once again "...all things (will) work together for good to them that love God..." Thankfully, I have an even greater promise after this life ends of an unimaginable, heavenly world free of pain, trauma, oppression, persecution, and separation. There will be peace, freedom, and joy like we have never experienced. Jesus cannot wait to introduce us to it.

Joel and I agree that in some ways my experience parallels that of Joseph in the Bible. Both Joseph and I were removed from a comfortable life with our family and thrust alone into an unknown world that we did not choose. We both endured adversity, trauma, and pain in our new land but over time the good outweighed the bad. Joseph was eventually reunited with his family, but I was not until I acquired the portrait of Matilde, my most prized possession. In the end God used both Joseph's and my circumstances for good as souls were saved and are still being saved because of the favor God extended to us. In comparison to Joseph, I may be insignificant in the eyes of man, but not in the eyes of God.

During the pandemic Joel rushed into the house from work advising me to go to his office and join a Zoom meeting online with Jody, the Guinn's- missionaries, and some of our Cuban ministers who were at various locations in Cuba. What an honor and a privilege that it was to be invited to interact with that elite group of people who are active in spreading the gospel to the nation of Cuba. I weep with joy every time I recall that day on a Cuban beach that I watched Jody baptize in Jesus Name those three ministers. I praise God that Jody has been so active in soliciting funds from UPCI pastors and setting up conferences for the UPCI in Cuba since 2010. I rejoice when I can watch on Facebook actual videos of activities in Cuba like the baptism of eight Cuban converts in Jesus Name in a spring in Artemisa, perhaps on land near land my family had owned. How amazing it is that ministers in Cuba have graduated from Purpose Institute or are currently enrolled in Purpose Institute classes in Cuba. All are answers God has given me for "Why?"

So, to Satan and his emissary Castro God has the last word: "But as for you, you meant evil against me; *but* God meant it for good, in order to bring it about as *it is* this day, to save many people alive. Genesis 50:20 NKJV

<u>REFERENCES</u>

Yannis, A., 2022. DE LA SIERRA NAMED COSMOS'CHAIRMAN (published 1983). [online] Nytimes.com. Available at: https://www.nytimes.com/1983/11/29/sports/de-la-sierra-named-cosmos-chairman.html [Accessed 12 May 2022].

Ballotpedia Refugee Act of 1980 https://ballotpedia.org/Refugee_Act_of_1980 [accessed 5/26/2022[1]].

Congressional Research Service. Immigration Parole (Humanitarian Parole). NoR46570. 10/15/2020. https://sgp.fas.org/crs/homesec/R46570.pdf [accessed 5/24/72[2]].

Cubagenweb.org.2021. *El Cabellero de Paris*. [online] Available at: http://www.cubagenweb.org/misc/paris.htm [Accessed 14 May 2022].

https://insightcuba.com/blog/2016/10/21/explore-vedado

Sierra, Rafael De la. *Life Is a Carousel: A Novel Inspired by a True Sory*. Bloomington, IN: AuthorHouse, 2005.

---

1.   https://ballotpedia.org/Refugee_Act_of_1980%20%5baccessed%205/26/2022

2.   https://sgp.fas.org/crs/homesec/R46570.pdf%20%5baccessed%205/24/72

About the Author

Maria Baro Wells is a homemaker. She is an alumnus of the University of Central Florida who majored in Elementary Education. She attends Path Apostolic Church, Titusville, Florida currently pastored by her son, Jody Wells. She is a mother to three children Jody, Stephanie, and Zachary.

Joel L. Wells Sr is a Licensed Mental Health Counselor. He has a BA degree in Psychology and an MA degree in Counseling. He is a published author.